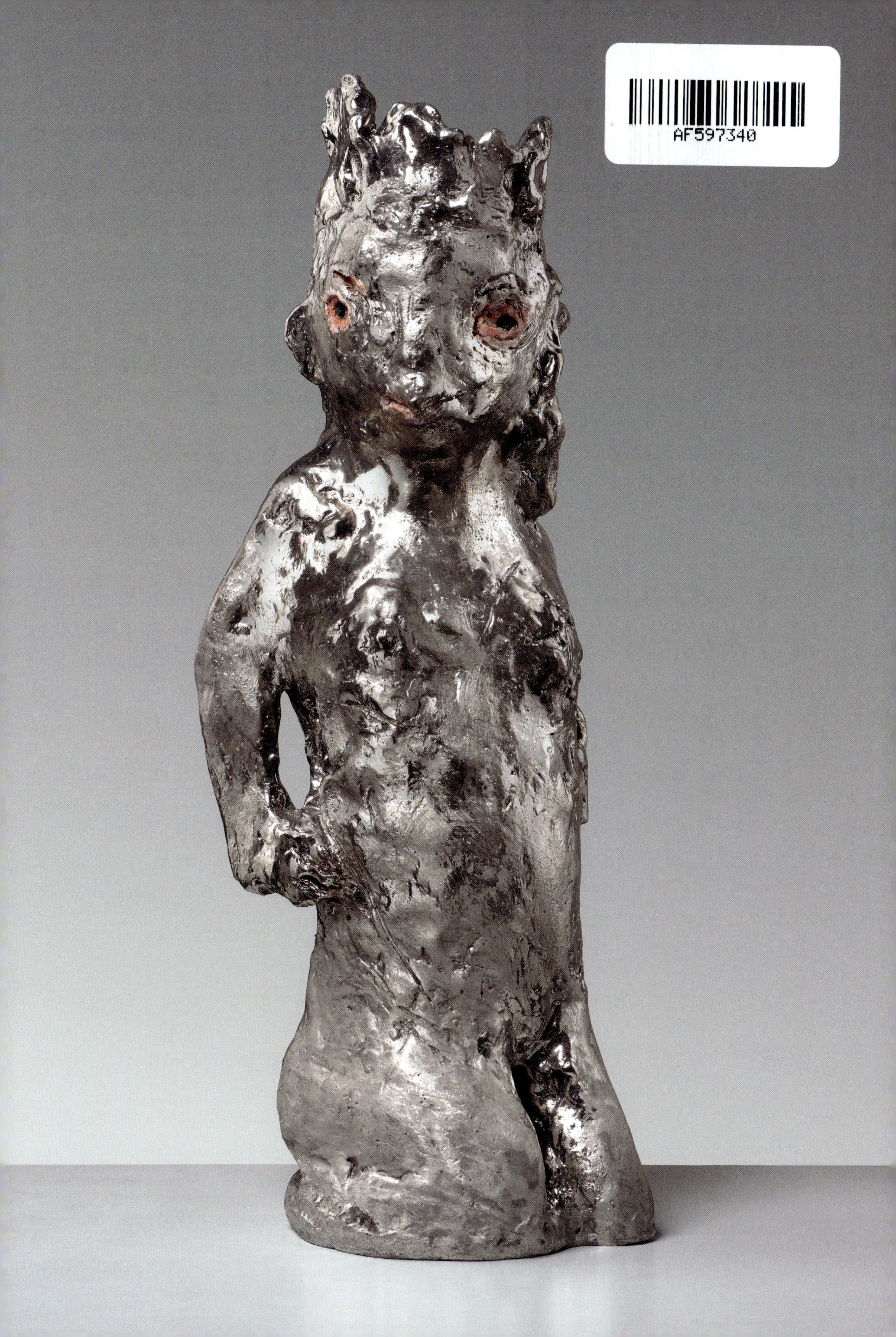

AF597340

LEIKO IKEMURA
MOMSTARS

Contemporary Fine Arts
Berlin 2024

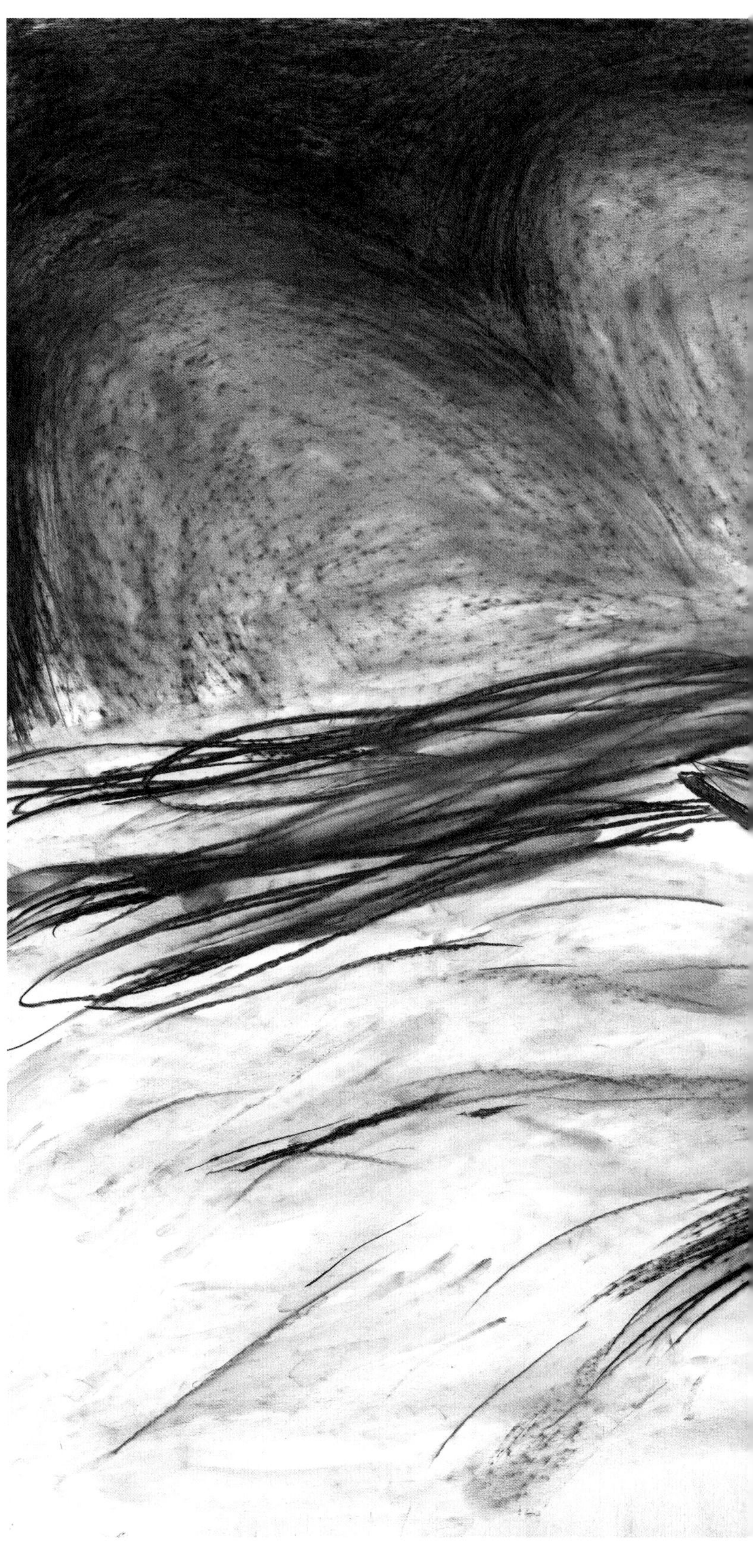

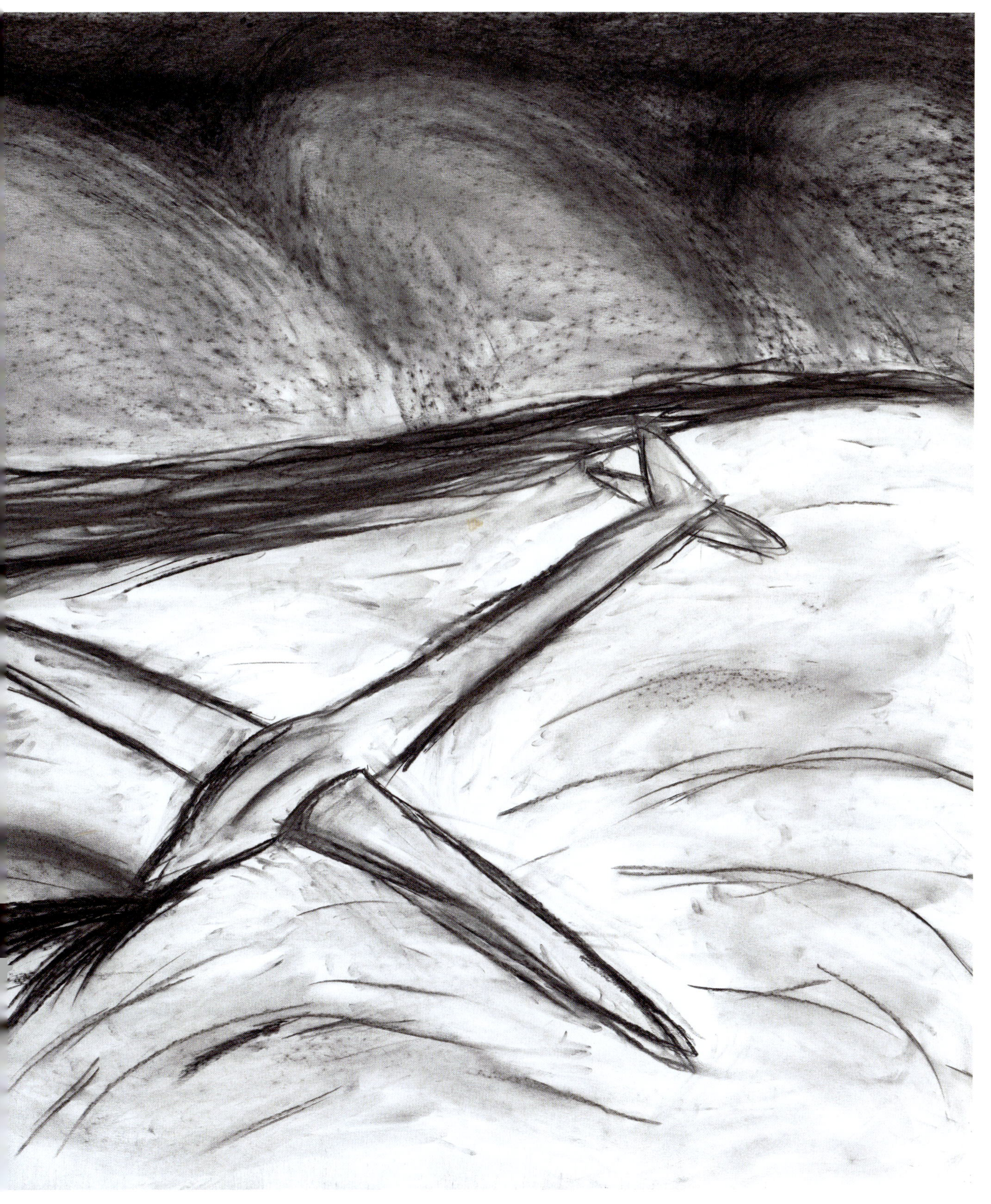

Landing, 1981

MONSTER... MOMS... MOMSTERS... ou plutôt MOMSTARS ! Voilà le titre de l'exposition imaginé avec une feuille de papier et un crayon, en quelques mots disposés sur une feuille comme une architecture de lettres. Née dans la ville de Tsu au Japon, Leiko Ikemura a commencé sa formation par la littérature à Osaka. Aujourd'hui, elle joue avec les lettres comme elle le fait avec les formes, en les fondant les unes dans les autres.

Nous nous retrouvons au dernier étage de la maison qu'elle habite, une grande pièce remplie de lumière dans un immeuble de Kreuzberg, entre Mitte et Kottbusser Tor. Tout autour de nous, des étagères basses à la façon de Barragán, débordant de livres et de disques. Un ensemble de vases de céramique blancs évoque des tableaux de Morandi, ou bien des corps immobiles. Des œuvres sont accrochées au mur et posées sur le sol, achetées à des artistes amis, ou bien fruits de rencontres et de coups de foudre artistiques. Et sur des socles, une collection d'animaux de laine portant à l'oreille le sigle de Steiff, une marque allemande de peluches fabriquées à la main qui suscite l'admiration de Leiko Ikemura et de son mari, l'architecte Philipp von Matt, auteur de la maison où l'on se trouve. Ces anciens jouets sont chargées des âmes des enfants qui ont joué avec eux.

Sur le sol devant nous, Leiko Ikemura est en train de construire le récit de l'exposition avec la maquette de l'espace de la galerie: au rez-de chaussée, des œuvres récentes, et à l'étage supérieur, un ensemble d'œuvres des années 1980 qu'elle continue elle-même de redécouvrir depuis ses expositions en 2019 au National Museum de Tokyo et au Kunstmuseum de Bâle. Cet accrochage révèle à la fois les évolutions formelles de ses recherches, et le troublant effet de persistance rétinienne que suscite également leur cohérence au fil des années.

« Guernica of our time » est l'un des plus grands tableaux de l'exposition, figure un point de départ pour toutes les œuvres récentes. C'est un précipité de peinture sombre, à peine éclairé par des taches, de vert et d'orange, quelques traits de bleu, d'orange et de rose, tels des feux d'artifice menaçants. Sur ce grand format horizontal, les coulures de peinture pourraient évoquer les lances de soldats de « la Bataille de San Romano » de Paolo Uccello. La toile de jute, tissée avec des fils épais, contribue encore au caractère ombrageux de la scène. « Pourquoi n'exige-t-on pas qu'ils s'arrêtent », se demande Leiko Ikemura comme un appel contre les guerres de ces dernières années ces dernières années. « Voilà ma réaction à l'état du monde aujourd'hui », ajoute-t-elle.

Quatre plus petits tableaux intitulés « Insomnia » accompagnent cette grande œuvre. Des images flottantes se devinent au fur et à mesure qu'elles nous échappent. Elles sont elles aussi illuminées d'extraordinaires variations de violets, de vert émeraude, de rouge foncé et de bruns. Leiko Ikemura a toujours œuvré entre abstraction et figuration, avec l'idée que l'observation de la nature se résume souvent à des ombres et des vibrations. On ne voit pas ce que les choses sont. D'où viennent alors ces visions de nuits sans sommeil ? « Le sommeil de la raison engendre des monstres », disait Goya, intitulant ainsi l'une de ses gravures de la série des « Caprices ». Leiko Ikemura parle à propos de ses peintures des pluies noires radioactives observées après les bombardements atomiques de Hiroshima et de Nagasaki. Il y a toujours chez elle une forte conscience écologique.

D'autres œuvres de la même époque présentent d'ailleurs des créatures, tout droit issues également de la peinture de Goya, toutes déformées avec leurs yeux exorbités. Elles sont debout sur des fonds jaunes et rouges, pleurant en marchant, les cheveux comme des branches d'arbres, tenant un chat bleu dans les bras, ou simplement face à nous, toutes surprises de nous voir les regarder. L'une d'entre elles, une « Goyesca », brandit dans sa main un petit personnage qu' elle s'apprête à dévorer, comme le « Saturne dévorant ses enfants » de Goya. Ces créatures ont aussi probablement croisé des yōkai sur leur chemin, ces êtres surnaturels du folklore japonais que Leiko Ikemura a bien connus à travers les récits de son enfance. Elle entretient avec le monde un rapport dans lequel l'animisme a sa place. Et de là à l'intelligence artificielle, il n'y a qu'un pas, remarque-t-elle.

Avec ses personnages, Leiko Ikemura s'inscrit dans ces nouvelles narrations, formalistes et fantastiques, que l'on a vu apparaitre dans la peinture depuis quelques années, et qu'elle définit elle-même en se comparant avec des artistes comme Susan Rothenberg, Nicole Eisenman, ou Cecily Brown. Il y a de nombreuses figures de femmes dans ses images, comme cette *pietà*, « big mom », peinte sur une toile de coton qui renforce la luminosité des couleurs. Sa silhouette, ses yeux bleus et sa longue chevelure se dessinent en quelques traits et quelques aplats de couleur. Et c'est une autre généalogie qu'elle nomme à propos de ces gestes, celle des rares femmes de l'expressionnisme abstrait, Lee Krasner, Joan Mitchell et Helen Frankenthaler, ou les artistes de Gutai, qui la ramènent, dit-elle encore, au geste de la calligraphie japonaise, et à la présence des corps dans la peinture.

Si elle parle volontiers de calligraphie, Leiko Ikemura pratique également la céramique, choisissant un médium après l'autre pour une période avant d'en changer. Deux « Rocket Girls », qui pourraient évoquer les sculptures de l'Américaine Kiki Smith, se tiennent accroupies. Le haut de leur crâne est ouvert, pour laisser le vide entrer en elle. Pour Leiko Ikemura, sculpter consiste d'abord à construire le vide. A la fois destructrices et nourricières, elles ont chacune une fusée sur le dos, à moins que ce ne soit un lézard, une forme phallique ou un petit avion.

C'est un destin unique que celui de Leiko Ikemura, artiste qui s'est toujours positionnée aux carrefours de l'histoire, en observatrice, avec la précision et l'incongruité d'un chat dans un rai de lumière. Élevée dans une petite ville du Japon, elle s'installe en Espagne en 1973, alors que Franco était encore au pouvoir, non pas à Madrid mais à Séville. Elle était à la recherche d'un temps perdu – l'histoire du Japon de ses origines ayant été détruits par la Seconde Guerre mondiale et par les bombardements nucléaires. Elle raconte aussi avoir trouvé en Andalousie de l'art vivant dans des églises et dans les rues. C'est là qu'elle découvre de Jose de Ribera, de Murillo, de Velasquez, de Goya… C'est là aussi, à la faveur de voyages à Madrid, qu'elle a connu l'œuvre de Picasso, de Miro et des surréalistes qui ont tant marqué son œuvre. Elle y a également appris le dessin et les recettes traditionnelles de la peinture à la tempera et à l'œuf, à laquelle elle mêle encore aujourd'hui ses pigments naturels qui lui procurent ses matités magnifiques. C'est à Séville enfin qu'elle a assisté à la mort de Franco et à la fin de la dictature espagnole.

Depuis l'Espagne, elle a entrepris de partir pour la Suisse, où elle a d'abord séjourné, avant de s'installer à Zurich en 1979 pour quatre ans. Ce pays était celui de la neutralité. Elle y a été témoin de mouvements de libération de la jeunesse. Un peu plus tard, elle a même passé une année entière dans les montagnes suisses: peut-être l'occasion de retrouver une intimité avec la nature présente dans son enfance japonaise – même si elle est une personne de la mer plus que des montagnes. A cet égard, les peintres japonais comme Hokusai, ou Hasegawa Tōhaku sont pour elle très importants, car leurs œuvres expriment ce rapport au monde animiste dans lequel les règnes se mêlent. A l'époque il n'y avait pas de musées d'art contemporain en Espagne; c'est à l'âge de 30 ans qu'elle a vu à Lucerne sa première exposition de Jannis Kounellis.

Ensuite, ce n'est pas pour Paris qu'elle est partie, comme l'avaient fait avant elle tant d'artistes de la modernité – elle adore les chats de Foujita –, mais pour l'Allemagne encore marquée par la Guerre Froide, peut-être toujours à la recherche inconsciente d'un lieu de mémoire. A Cologne d'abord, en 1985, la scène artistique était dynamique, mais dominée par des hommes de la génération de la Mülheimer Freiheit. L'une des très rares femmes dans ce paysage, Leiko Ikemura s'intéresse plutôt aux artistes italiens de la Transavangarde comme Francesco Clemente qu'elle a rencontré plus tard ou au danois Per Kirkeby.

A l'étage de l'exposition, consacré à des œuvres des années 1980, un autre dessin monumental répond à « Guernica of our time » (2023), comme un écho direct de cet hommage à Picasso. Le format est semblable et le cri a la même puissance. Une tonalité violente apparaît également dans une série de dessins. Il ne s'agit pas seulement de contes cruels de l'enfance. L'œuvre de Leiko Ikemura est aussi marquée par l'atmosphère de l'après-guerre lorsqu'elle vivait au Japon, dont elle a retrouvé l'empreinte dans l'Allemagne de cette époque.

Menaçante et protectrice, avec son drôle de fond bleu, la peinture intitulée « Araignée » pourrait trouver une résonnance dans le tableau de Max Ernst, « L'ange du foyer », qui désigne les ravages du franquisme – mais dans une version plus terrienne que l'oiseau du surréaliste. Et ce motif pourrait aussi aujourd'hui être rapproché des sculptures de Louise Bourgeois, « Maman ». Leiko Ikemura n'a-t-elle pas intitulé son exposition « Momstars » ? Dans ces années 1980, Leiko Ikemura peint de façon assez différente de ce qu'elle a fait avant et après. On lui reproche alors, raconte-t-elle, d'utiliser par trop les outils du dessin en peinture: ses effets de matités et de transparences, et son trait précis. Elle s'essaye à la peinture acrylique par exemple dans son triptyque, « Yokai night », de 1985, une sarabande de chimères et de créatures tournoyant autour de la tête d'un âne de profil. Il y a une dimension très archaïque dans ce tableau, qui semble réunir chez elle l'Espagne de Goya et l'expressionnisme allemand de Kirchner avec, dans un panneau plus contemplatif, un penseur au pied d'un arbre.

En 1981, elle dessine un étrange avion qui atterrit sur le sol. Peut-être s'est-il écrasé. On pense plutôt à celui de Joseph Beuys, accidenté dans un désert où il a été sauvé par des Tatars. C'est ce qu'il raconte. Et c'est l'un des fondements de sa mythologie. Leiko Ikemura s'est toujours intéressée à cet artiste qui a cohabité pendant trois jours avec un coyote pour sa performance « I like America and America likes me ». Elle l'a rencontré, avec un critique d'art qui venait d'écrire sur lui. Puis elle est retournée le voir pour lui offrir un dessin d'elle: un homme plantant un arbre, hommage aux 7000 chênes que Beuys a plantés à Kassel pour la Documenta 7 en 1982. Cet avion se rapproche évidemment de ceux que portent sur leur dos les « Rocket Girls » en cire et en bronze, des avions magiques, ambivalents, qui dessinent un trait entre la terre et le ciel.

Juste après la chute du Mur de Berlin, en 1990, Leiko Ikemura s'installe là, car elle a été nommée professeure de peinture à la Hochschule der Künste. Toujours tel le chat, dont elle dit parfois qu'il s'abrite en elle, elle s'est à nouveau posée dans un lieu où l'histoire était sensible dans la rue, sur la peau des murs et dans l'allure des passants. Une ville en transition permanente, dont les géographies contemporaines n'ont plus rien à voir avec celles de son arrivée. A l'image de son travail, d'une forme à l'autre.

Anaël Pigeat
Berlin / Paris, Janvier 2024

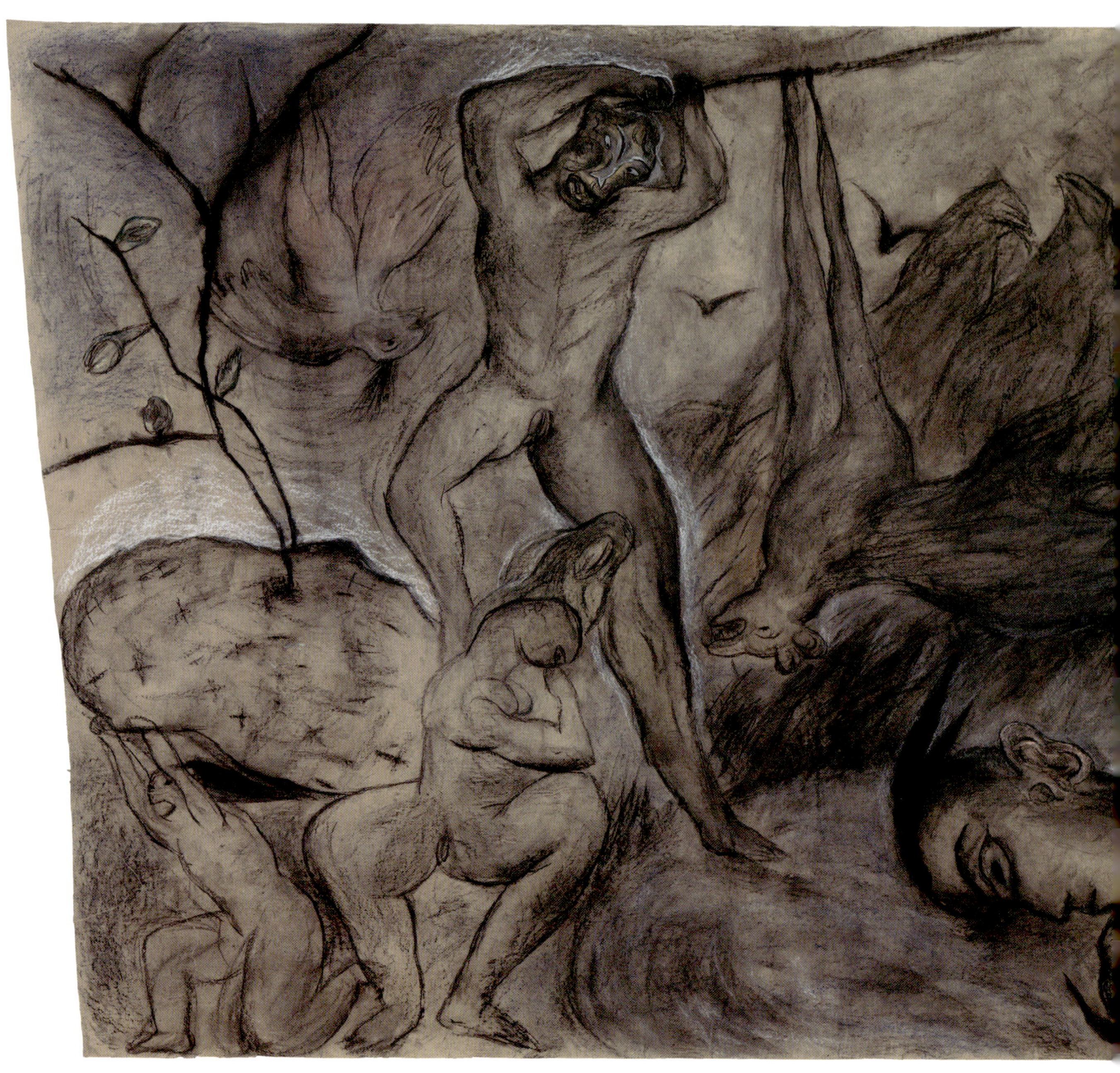

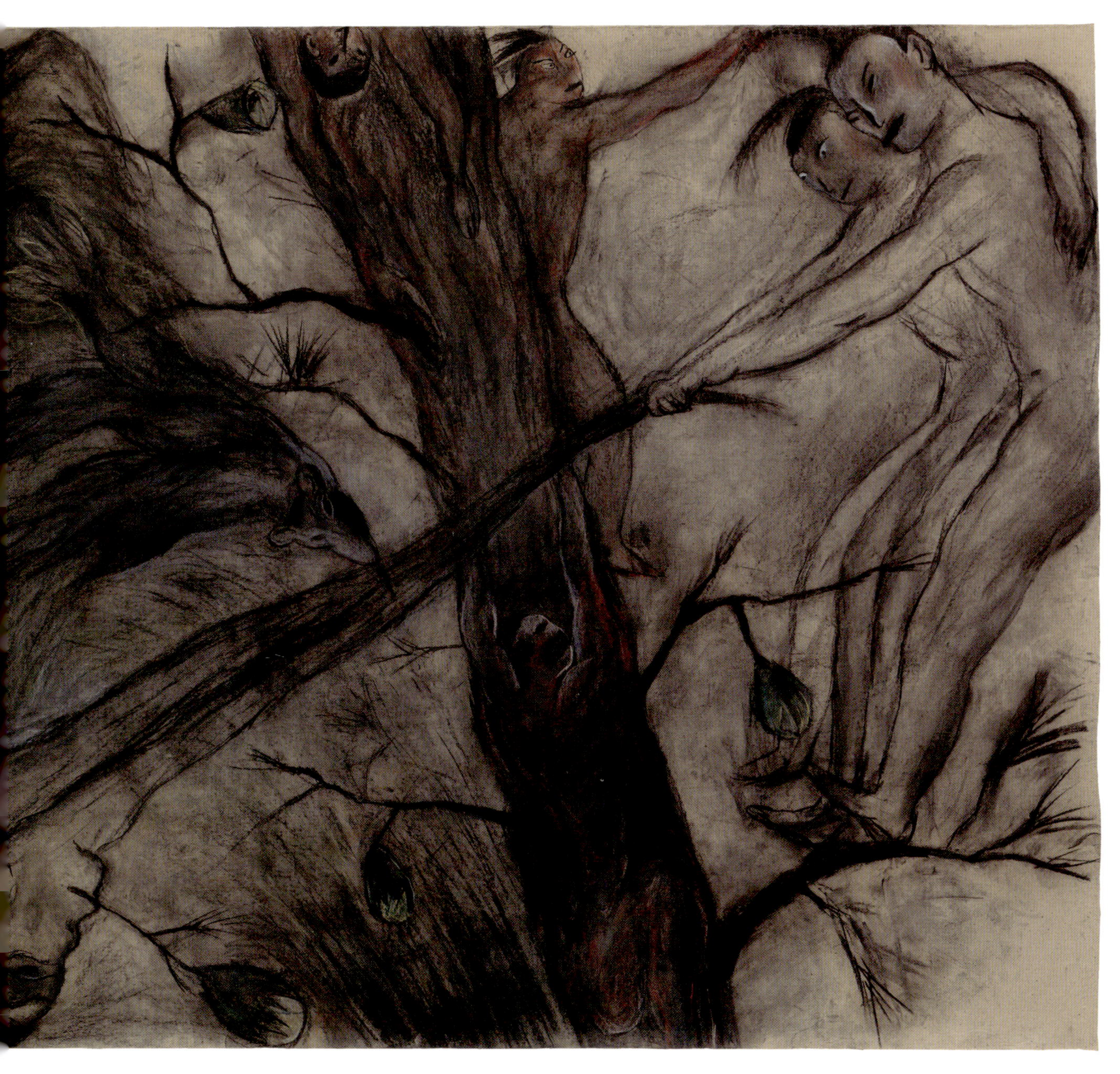

Yokais, 1983

MONSTER... MOMS... MOMSTERS... oder besser MOMSTARS! Der Titel der Ausstellung ist schon einmal angedacht, auf einem Stück Papier mit einem Bleistift und einigen wenigen Worten, auf dem Blatt ausgerichtet wie eine Architektur aus Buchstaben. Geboren in der Stadt Tsu in Japan, begann Leiko Ikemura ihre Ausbildung mit einem Literaturstudium in Osaka. Heute spielt sie mit den Buchstaben wie mit den Formen und lässt beide ineinander verschmelzen.

Wir treffen uns im obersten Stockwerk des Hauses, das sie bewohnt, einem großen lichtdurchfluteten Raum in einem Kreuzberger Gebäude, zwischen Mitte und Kottbusser Tor. Rings um uns, voller überbordender Bücher und Schallplatten, niedrige Regale à la Barragán. Ein Ensemble weißer Keramikvasen erinnert an Bilder von Morandi oder an reglose Körper. Aufgehängt an den Wänden und auf dem Boden aufgestellt sind Werke, die sie von befreundeten Künstlern erworben hat oder die ihr als Erträge künstlerischer Begegnungen und Blitzverliebtheiten zugewachsen sind. Dazu auf Sockeln eine Sammlung handgefertigter Plüschtiere mit dem Steiff-Knopf im Ohr. Objekte der Bewunderung Leiko Ikemuras und ihres Lebensgefährten Philipp von Matt, dem Architekten des Hauses. Die alten Stofftiere bewahren noch die Seelen der Kinder, die einst mit ihnen spielten.

Auf dem Boden vor uns entwirft Leiko Ikemura anhand eines Modells des Galerieraums den Ablauf der Ausstellung: im Erdgeschoss jüngst entstandene Werke und im Obergeschoss ein Ensemble von Arbeiten aus den 1980er Jahren, die sie seit ihren Ausstellungen 2019 im National Museum in Tokio und im Kunstmuseum Basel selber neu für sich entdeckt. Die Hängung offenbart die formalen Entwicklungen ihrer Forschungen. Sie erzeugt dabei ein beunruhigendes Nachbild, das aus dem die Jahre übergreifenden Zusammenhang entsteht.

»Guernica of our time« ist eines der größten Bilder in der Ausstellung und bietet einen Ausgangspunkt auch für die Werke der jüngeren Zeit. Da herrscht ein Andrang dunkler Farbe, kaum gelichtet durch rosa, grüne oder orange Flecken; Pinselstriche in Blau, Orange und Rosa wirken wie unheilkündende Feuerwerke. Die Farbrinnsale auf diesem großen Querformat könnten an die Lanzen der Soldaten in Paolo Uccellos »Schlacht von San Romano« denken lassen. Aus kräftigen Fasern gewoben, trägt die Juteleinwand zusätzlich zur beängstigenden Ausstrahlung der Kampfszene bei. »Warum wird nicht verlangt, dass sie aufhören«, fragt sich Leiko Ikemura in einem Appell gegen die Kriege, die in den vergangenen Jahren die Welt heimsuchen. »Soweit meine Reaktion auf den Zustand der heutigen Welt«, fügt sie hinzu.

Vier kleinere, »insomnia« betitelte Bilder gehen mit dieser großen Arbeit einher. Abstrakt anmutend, sind schwebende Gebilde zu erahnen, die sich uns im gleichen Maße wieder entziehen. Auch sie sind durchleuchtet von außergewöhnlichen Farbvariationen in Violett, Smaragdgrün, Dunkelrot und Braun. Leiko Ikemura arbeitet seit jeher zwischen Abstraktion und Figuration, aus dem Gedanken heraus, dass die Beobachtung der Natur über Schatten und Schwingungen oft nicht hinausgelangt. Man sieht nicht, was die Dinge sind. Woher kommen nun diese Visionen schlafloser Nächte? »Der Schlaf der Vernunft gebiert Ungeheuer«, meinte Goya und betitelte so eines seiner »Caprichos«. Mit Blick auf diese Gemälde spricht Leiko Ikemura von den radioaktiven Regenfällen, die nach den nuklearen Bombardierungen von Hiroshima und Nagasaki beobachtet wurden. Ein starkes ökologisches Bewusstsein war ihr immer gegeben.

Weitere Werke aus derselben Zeit zeigen übrigens – ebenfalls geradewegs der Malerei

Goyas entsprungen – Kreaturen, ganz ungestalt mit ihren aus den Höhlen tretenden Augen. Aufrecht vor gelbem und rotem Grund, weinen sie im Gehen mit wie Baumzweige aufgestellten Haaren, halten eine blaue Katze in den Armen oder stehen einfach vor uns, davon überrascht, dass wir sie anschauen. Eine Figur, wie eine »Goyesca« anmutend, schwenkt in ihrer Hand eine kleine Figur, die sie aufzufressen sich anschickt, wie der Gott in Goyas »Saturn verschlingt seine Kinder«. Vermutlich sind diese Kreaturen auch Yōkai über den Weg gelaufen, den übernatürlichen Geschöpfen aus dem japanischen Volksglauben, die Leiko Ikemura in den Erzählungen ihrer Kindheit kennengelernt hat. Sie unterhält eine Beziehung zur Welt, in der der Animismus durchaus seinen Platz hat – die Vorstellung also, in der auch Objekte belebt sind. Von dort bis hin zur Künstlichen Intelligenz, merkt sie an, ist es nur noch ein Schritt.

Mit diesen Figuren reiht sich Leiko Ikemura in die neuen formalistischen und fantastischen Narrationen ein, die man seit ein paar Jahren in der Malerei auftauchen sieht, und sie widerspricht auch nicht, als ich sie mit Susan Rothenberg, Nicole Eisenman oder Cecily Brown in Beziehung setze. Zahlreiche Frauengestalten treten in ihren Bildern auf, eine Pietà etwa mit dem Titel »big mom«, gemalt auf Nessel, der die Leuchtkraft der Farben verstärkt. Die Silhouette, die blauen Augen und das lange Haar zeichnen sich in wenigen Strichen und Farbflächen ab. Mit diesem Gestus ruft die Künstlerin eine weitere Genealogie auf, nämlich die der seltener erwähnten Frauen des abstrakten Expressionismus, Lee Krasner, Joan Mitchell und Helen Frankenthaler, oder auch der Künstlergruppe Gutai, durch die sie, wie sie ergänzt, zur Geste der japanischen Kalligrafie und zur Präsenz der Körper in der Malerei zurückgekehrt ist.

Spricht Leiko Ikemura gern von Kalligrafie, so praktiziert sie gleichzeitig auch in den verschiedenen Medien der Bildhauerei und mit Keramik, wobei sie sich nach einem Medium phasenweise einem anderen zuwendet, bevor sie auch dieses wieder verlässt.

So finden sich in der Ausstellung zwei kauernde »Rocket Girls«, die, auch wenn Leiko Ikemura nicht die Absicht verfolgt hatte, an die Skulpturen der Amerikanerin Kiki Smith denken lassen. Ihre Schädeldecken sind offen, um die Leere in sie aufzunehmen. Für Leiko Ikemura besteht bildhauerische Arbeit zuallererst darin, der Leere Gestalt zu geben. Zerstörerisch und nährend zugleich, tragen diese Figuren auf dem Rücken jeweils eine Rakete – falls es sich nicht doch um eine Eidechse, eine phallische Form oder ein kleines Flugzeug handeln sollte.

Es ist schon ein einzigartiger Lebensweg, den die Künstlerin Leiko Ikemura gegangen ist, die sich immer an den Kreuzungen der Geschichte positioniert hat, auf denen sie, mit der Präzision und Unbotmäßigkeit einer Katze in einem Sonnenstrahl, als Beobachterin Platz nimmt. Aufgewachsen in einer japanischen Kleinstadt, ließ sie sich 1973 in Spanien nieder, nicht in Madrid, wo Franco weitaus präsenter war, sondern in Sevilla. Sie war auf der Suche nach einer verlorenen Zeit – denn die Geschichte ihrer Heimat Japan war zerstört durch den Zweiten Weltkrieg und die nuklearen Bombardierungen. Auch erzählt sie, in Andalusien lebendige Kunst in Kirchen und auf den Straßen gefunden zu haben. In Spanien begegnete sie Bildern von José de Ribera, Murillo, Velázquez, Goya und machte im Zuge ihrer Reisen nach Madrid auch Bekanntschaft mit den Werken Picassos, Mirós und der Surrealisten, von denen ihr eigenes Werk so stark beeinflusst wurde. Dort lernte sie außerdem das Zeichnen und die traditionellen Zubereitungen der Eitemperafarben, denen sie noch heute die natürlichen Pigmente beimengt, aus denen sie ihre wunderbaren matten Texturen kreiert. In Sevilla erlebte sie schließlich den Tod Francos und das Ende der spanischen Diktatur.

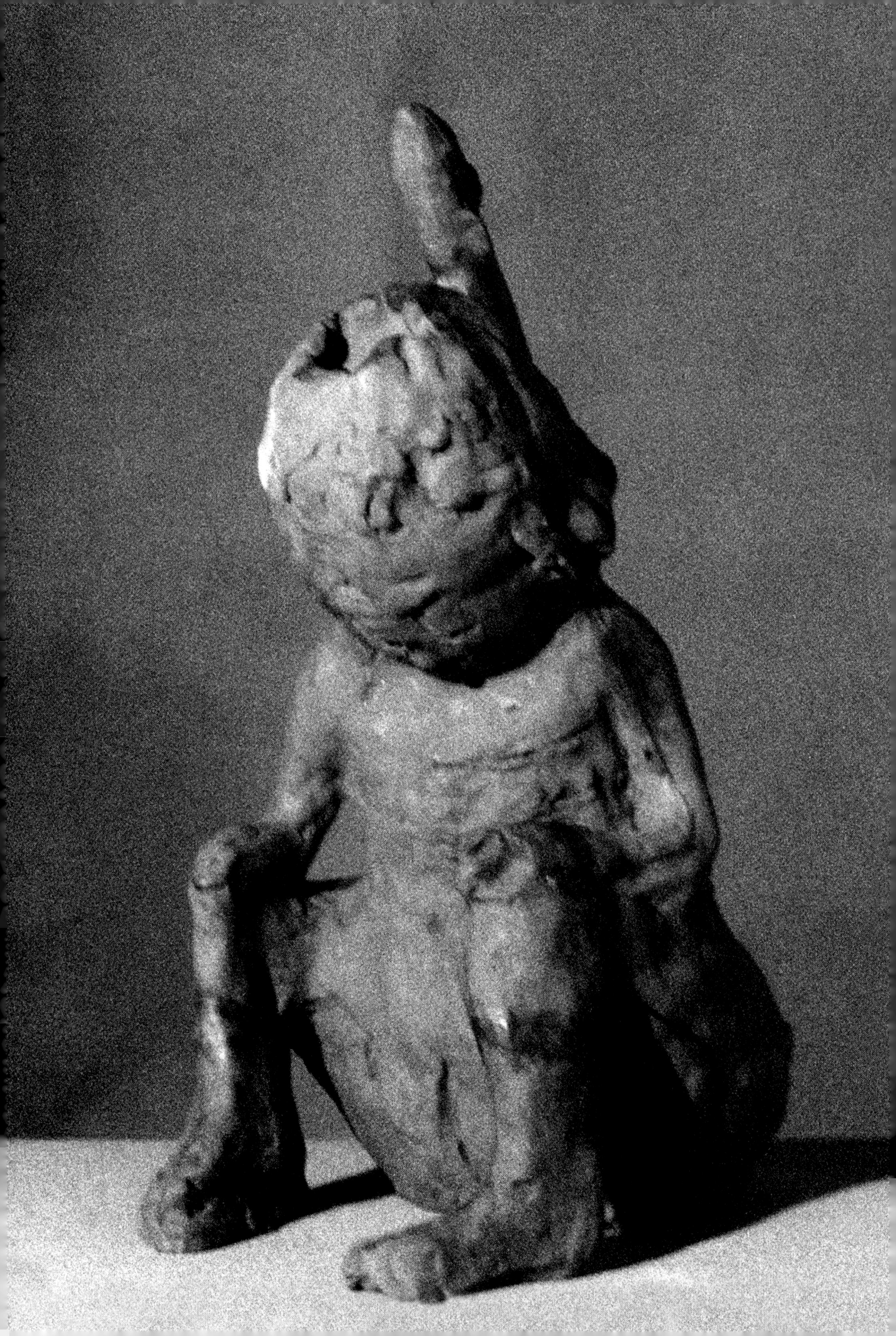

Von Spanien aus wagte sie den Aufbruch in die Schweiz, wo sie sich zunächst zeitweise aufhielt, um sich 1979 für vier Jahre in Zürich niederzulassen. Die Schweiz war das Land der Neutralität, hier erlebte sie die Jugendrevolten. Etwas später verbrachte sie sogar ein ganzes Jahr in den Schweizer Bergen, eine Gelegenheit, die Nähe zur Natur wiederzufinden, die in ihrer japanischen Kindheit sehr gegenwärtig war – auch wenn sie eine Frau der Meere eher als der Berge ist. In dieser Hinsicht sind ihr japanische Maler wie Hokusai oder Hasegawa Tōhaku sehr wichtig, bringen deren Werke doch die Beziehung zur animistischen Welt zum Ausdruck, in der die Reiche sich vermischen. Damals gab es in Spanien kein Museum für zeitgenössische Kunst; im Alter von dreißig Jahren sah sie in Luzern ihre erste Ausstellung von Jannis Kounellis.

Danach ging sie nicht etwa nach Paris, wie viele Künstler noch in der Moderne – sie schwärmt für die Katzenbilder von Foujita –, sondern ins seinerzeit vom Kalten Krieg geprägte Deutschland, vielleicht nach wie vor auf der unbewussten Suche nach einem Erinnerungsort. Zuerst Köln: 1985 war dort die Kunstszene dynamisch, wurde aber von Männern beherrscht – der Generation der Mülheimer Freiheit. Als eine der sehr wenigen Frauen in dieser Landschaft interessierte sich Leiko Ikemura aber eher für die italienischen Künstler der Transavantgarde wie Francesco Clemente, den sie später persönlich kennenlernte, oder für den Dänen Per Kirkeby.

Im Obergeschoss der Ausstellung, das den Werken der 1980er Jahre gewidmet ist, bildet eine monumentale Zeichnung aus dem Jahr 1983 ein direktes Echo zur Picasso-Hommage »Guernica of our time« (2023). Das Format ist ein ähnliches, und der Schrei hat dieselbe Kraft. Eine Auseinandersetzung mit Gewalt zeigt sich auch in einer Reihe von annähernd figurativen Zeichnungen. Es sind nicht nur grausame Erzählungen aus der Kindheit. Ihr Werk ist geprägt von der Atmosphäre der Nachkriegszeit, die sie in Japan verbrachte. Leiko Ikemura fand deren Spur im Deutschland jener Jahre wieder.

So bedrohlich wie beschützend, könnte das Bild mit dem Titel »Spider« ein Widerschein von Max Ernsts Gemälde »Der Hausengel« sein, welches die Verheerungen des Franquismus schildert – freilich in einer irdischeren Version als es der Vogel des Surrealisten tut. Auch ließe sie sich das Motiv heute mit Louise Bourgeois' »Maman«-Skulpturen vergleichen. Hat Leiko Ikemura ihrer Ausstellung nicht den Titel »Momstars« gegeben?

In den 1980er Jahren malt Leiko Ikemura ganz anders als zuvor und danach. Damals, berichtet sie, wurde ihr vorgeworfen, in der Malerei allzu häufig zeichnerisches Instrumentarium einzusetzen: ihr Spiel mit matten Texturen und Transparenzen und ihr präziser Strich. Sie versucht sich an der Acrylmalerei, zum Beispiel in dem Triptychon »Yokai night« von 1985, einer Sarabande von Schimären und Kreaturen, die einen Eselskopf im Profil umtanzen. Es liegt etwas sehr Archaisches in diesem dreiteiligen Gemälde, das Goyas Spanien mit dem deutschen Expressionismus eines Kirchner zusammenzubringen scheint und auf einer kontemplativ gehaltenen Tafel einen Denkenden zu Füßen eines Baumes zeigt.

1981 zeichnet sie ein merkwürdiges Flugzeug, das auf dem Boden landet. Vielleicht ist es abgestürzt. Man denkt durchaus an dasjenige des in der Tundra verunglückten Joseph Beuys der dort von Tataren geborgen wurde. So zumindest schilderte er eines der Fundamente seiner Mythologie. Leiko Ikemura interessiert sich seit jeher für den Künstler, der für seine Performance »I like America and America likes me« drei Tage mit einem Kojoten zusammenlebte. Sie lernte ihn kennen, zusammen mit einem Kunstkritiker, der gerade etwas über ihn geschrieben hatte. Dann besuchte sie ihn noch einmal, um ihm eine Zeichnung zu schenken, die er behalten hat: ein Mann, der einen Baum pflanzt, Hommage an die 7.000 Eichen, die Beuys 1982 für die Documenta 7 gepflanzt hat. Auch gleicht dieses Flugzeug natürlich denen, die die »Rocket Girls« aus Wachs bzw. Bronze auf dem Rücken tragen: magische, ambivalente Flugzeuge, die einen Strich zwischen Erde und Himmel zeichnen.

1990, kurz nach dem Mauerfall, zog Leiko Ikemura nach Berlin, da sie auf eine Professur für Malerei an die Hochschule der Bildenden Künste berufen worden war. Noch immer wie die Katze, die, wie sie manchmal sagt, in ihr wohnt, hat sie sich erneut an einem Ort niedergelassen, an dem die Geschichte auf der Straße zu spüren ist, auf der Außenhaut der Mauern und im Verhalten der Passanten. Eine Stadt im ständigen Übergang, deren heutige Geografie sich von der ihrer Ankunftszeit weiterentwickelt hat. Ganz wie ihre Arbeit – von einer Form zur nächsten.

Anaël Pigeat
Berlin / Paris, Januar 2024

Rocket Girl I+II, 2023

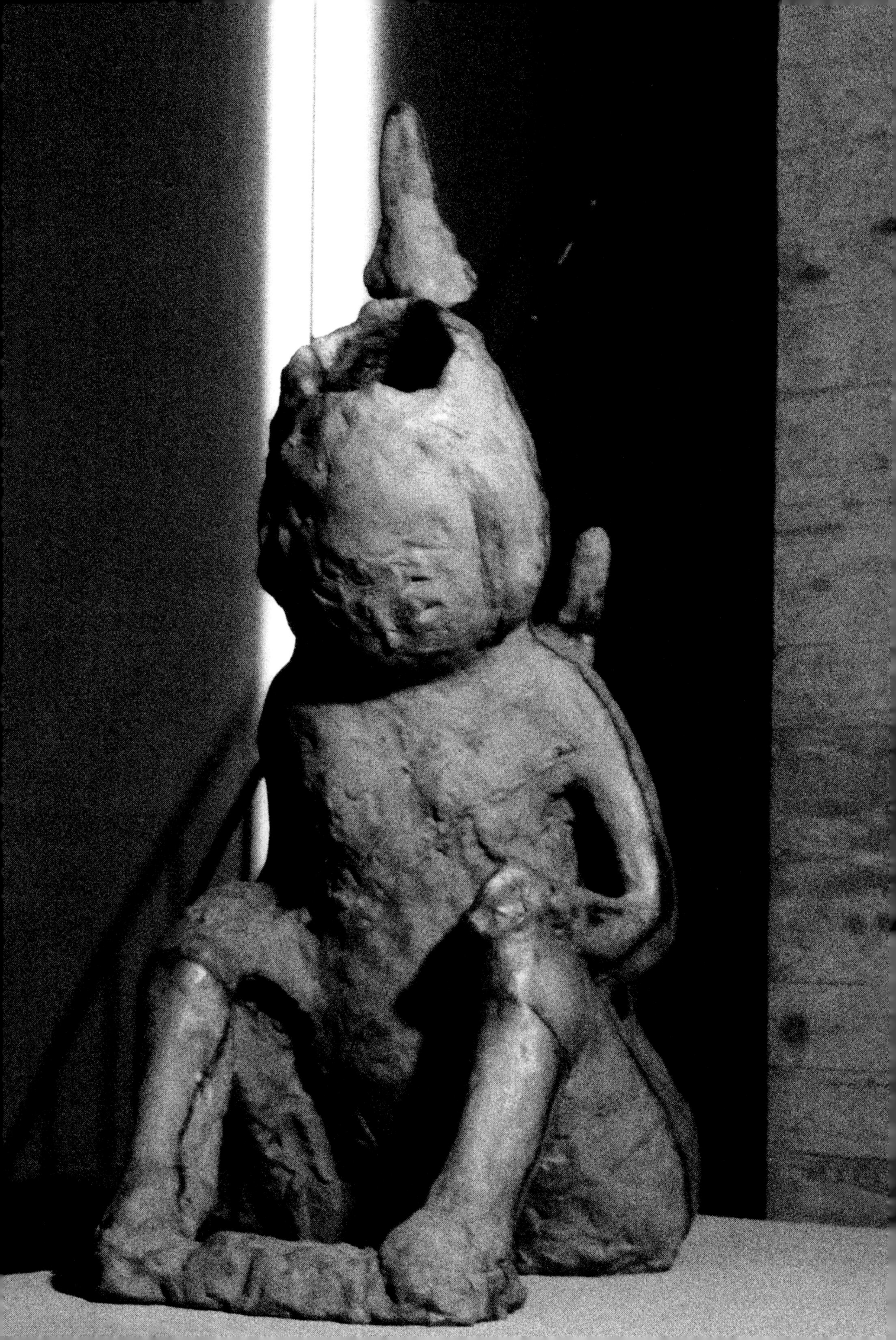

MONSTER... MOMS... MOMSTERS... or rather MOMSTARS! So that's how the exhibition title is conceived, with a piece of paper and a pencil, a few words laid out on the sheet like an architecture of letters. Born in Tsu, Japan, Leiko Ikemura started by studying literature in Osaka. Today, she plays with letters as she does with forms, blending them into each other.

We meet on the top floor of her house, a large, light-filled room in a building in Kreuzberg, between Mitte and Kottbusser Tor. All around us, low Barragán-style shelves overflowing with books and records. A group of white ceramic vases evoke paintings by Morandi, or immobile bodies. Works hang on the wall and are placed on the floor, purchased from artist friends, acquired in chance encounters or moments of spontaneous enthusiasm. And on pedestals, a collection of plush animals, with the Steiff button in ear, a German brand of handmade cuddly toys much admired by Leiko Ikemura and her partner, the architect Philipp von Matt, who designed the house. These old toys are charged with the souls of the children who once played with them.

On the floor in front of us, Ikemura is constructing the narrative of the exhibition using a model of the gallery space: on the ground floor, recent works, and on the upper floor, a group of pieces from the 1980s that she herself has been continuously rediscovering since her 2019 exhibitions at the National Museum in Tokyo and the Kunstmuseum in Basel. This hanging unveils both the formal developments in her researches and the troubling effect of retinal persistence induced by their coherence over the years.

"Guernica of our time" is one of the biggest of these paintings and provides a starting point for the more recent works. It is a precipitate of dark paint, barely illuminated by patches of pink, green and orange, a few dashes of blue, orange and pink, like threatening fireworks. On this large horizontal format, the drips of paint might recall the lances of the soldiers in Paolo Uccello's "The Battle of San Romano." The burlap, woven with thick threads, further heightens the shadowy character of the war scene. "Why isn't anyone demanding that they stop," asks Ikemura, in a plead against the wars that have ravaged the world in recent years. "That's it for my reaction to the state of the world today," she adds.

Four smaller paintings entitled "insomnia" go along with this large work. They seem abstract, almost floating. They escape us. They too are lit up by extraordinary variations of violet, emerald green, dark red and brown. Ikemura has always worked between abstraction and figuration, with the idea that observing nature often boils down to shadows and vibrations. We don't see what things are. So where do these visions of sleepless nights come from? "The sleep of reason produces monsters," said Goya in his title for one of the prints in his "Caprichos" series. Speaking of these paintings, Ikemura mentions the radioactive black rain that fell after the atomic bombings of Hiroshima and Nagasaki. There is always a strong ecological awareness in her work.

Other works from the same period feature creatures that also might have sprung up straight out of Goya's paintings, all deformed with bulging eyes. They are upright against yellow and red backgrounds, crying as they walk, their hair like tree branches, carrying a blue cat in their arms, maybe, or simply facing us, surprised to see us looking at them. One of them, "Goyesca", is holding up a small figure that it is about to devour, like Goya's "Saturn Devouring His Son". These creatures have probably also crossed paths with *yōkai*, the supernatural creatures of Japanese folklore that Ikemura came to know in the stories of her childhood. She has a relationship with the world in which animism has its place, the idea that objects are also alive. And so, as she points out, it's only a short step from this to artificial intelligence.

With her characters, Ikemura aligns herself with the new formalistic and fantastical narratives that have appeared in painting over recent years, and she doesn't object when I associate her with the likes of Susan Rothenberg, Nicole Eisenman, or Cecily Brown. There are many female figures in her images, as in her pietà, titled "big mom", painted on a cotton canvas which enhances the luminosity of the colours. Her form, blue eyes and long hair are outlined in a few strokes and a few tints of colour. And in these gestures, she now evokes another genealogy, that of the small band of women abstract expressionists, Lee Krasner, Joan Mitchell and Helen Frankenthaler, or the artists of Gutai, who take her back, she says, to the gesture of Japanese calligraphy, and to the presence of bodies in painting.

While Leiko Ikemura enjoys talking about calligraphy, she simultaneously engages in various forms of sculpture, such as ceramics or bronze. There are two "Rocket Girls" in the show, that could bring to mind the sculptures of the American artist Kiki Smith. The tops of their skulls are open, to let the emptiness in. For Ikemura, sculpting is first and foremost about giving form to emptiness. Both destructive and nurturing, these figures each have a rocket on their back, unless it's a lizard, a phallic shape or a small aeroplane.

It has been a unique destiny. The artist Ikemura has always positioned herself at the crossroads of history, as an observer, with the precision and incongruity of a cat in a ray of light. Brought up in a small town in Japan, she moved to Spain in 1973, while Franco was still in power. Not to Madrid but to Seville. She was searching for a time believed to be lost – the Japan of her ancestors was cut off by the Second World War and the nuclear bomb. She also speaks of finding living art in the churches and streets of Andalusia. It was there that she picked up her knowledge of Spanish Baroque art, of Jose de Ribera, of Velasquez , Murillo and Goya. It was also there, on trips to Madrid, that she got acquainted with works of Picasso, Miró and the Surrealists who had such an impact on her. And it was there that she learned drawing and the traditional technique of tempera painting – indeed, she still uses egg to bind her natural pigments today, which explains her magnificent matt tones. It was in Seville that she witnessed the death of Franco and the end of the Spanish dictatorship.

From Spain, she ventured to Switzerland, where she spent time before settling in Zurich in 1979. She lived there for your years. This was a country synonymous with neutrality. It was there that she witnessed youth liberation movements. A little later, she even spent a whole year in the Swiss mountains – a chance to rediscover an intimacy with nature that was present in her Japanese childhood, even if she is more of a sea person than a mountain person. In this respect, Japanese painters such as Hokusai and Hasegawa Tōhaku are very important to her, because their works express this relationship with the animistic world in which the kingdoms intermingle. At the time, there were no contemporary art museums in Spain; it was at the age of 30 that she saw her first exhibition by Jannis Kounellis in Lucerne.

When she left, it was not to go to Paris, like all those modernists before her – she loves Foujita's cats – but to Germany, still marked by the Cold War. Maybe she was still unconsciously searching for a place of memory. It was 1985 and the art scene in Cologne was dynamic, if dominated by men: the Mülheimer Freiheit generation. One of the very few women in this world, Ikemura was more interested in the Italian artists of the Transavanguardia, such as Francesco Clemente, whom she later met, and the Danish painter Per Kirkeby.

On the second floor of the exhibition, devoted to works from the 1980s, a monumental drawing from 1983 responds to the "Guernica of our time" (2023), like a direct echo of this homage to Picasso. The format is similar, and the scream has the same power. A violent tone also appears in a series of figurative drawings. These are not just cruel tales of childhood. Her work is influenced by the atmosphere of the post-war period that she spent in Japan. Leiko Ikemura found its imprint in Germany at that time.

Threatening and protective, with its strange blue background, the painting titled "Spider" could resonate with Max Ernst's work "The Angel of the Home," which refers to the ravages of Francoism – but in a more earthy version than the Surrealist's bird. Today it could also be compared to Louise Bourgeois's "Maman" sculptures. Didn't Ikemura title her exhibition "Momstars"?

Ikemura's paintings of the 1980s differ from what she did before and after. She was criticised, she recalls, for using too many tools of drawing in painting – her effects of mattness and transparency, and her precise line. She tried her hand at acrylic paint, for example, in her 1985 triptych "Yokai night", a saraband of chimeras and childlike creatures whirling around the head of a donkey in profile. There is a very archaic dimension to this painting, which seems to bring together the Spain of Goya and the German Expressionism of Kirchner with, in a more contemplative panel, a thinker at the foot of a tree.

In 1981, Ikemura drew a strange aeroplane landing. Possibly crashing. We think more of Joseph Beuys's plane, which crashed in the Crimea, where he was saved by Tatars. That, anyway, is how Beuys told it. And it is one of the foundations of his mythology. Ikemura has always been interested in this artist, who spent three days cohabiting with a coyote for his performance "I like America and America likes me." She met him with an art critic who had just written about him. Then she went back to see him to give him her drawing that he then kept: a man planting a tree, in tribute to the 7,000 oak trees that Beuys planted in Kassel for Documenta 7 in 1982. And this aeroplane is obviously similar to the ones carried on their backs by the "Rocket Girls" – magical, ambivalent aeroplanes that draw a line between earth and sky.

Just after the fall of the Wall in 1990, Ikemura moved to Berlin because she had been appointed professor at the Hochschule der Künste. Again, like the cat that she says sometimes lurks inside her, she once again settled in a place where history was palpable in the street, on the skin of the walls and in the gait of passers-by. A city in constant transition, whose contemporary geographies have evolved from the time of her arrival. Like her work, going from one form to another.

Anaël Pigeat
Berlin / Paris, January 2024

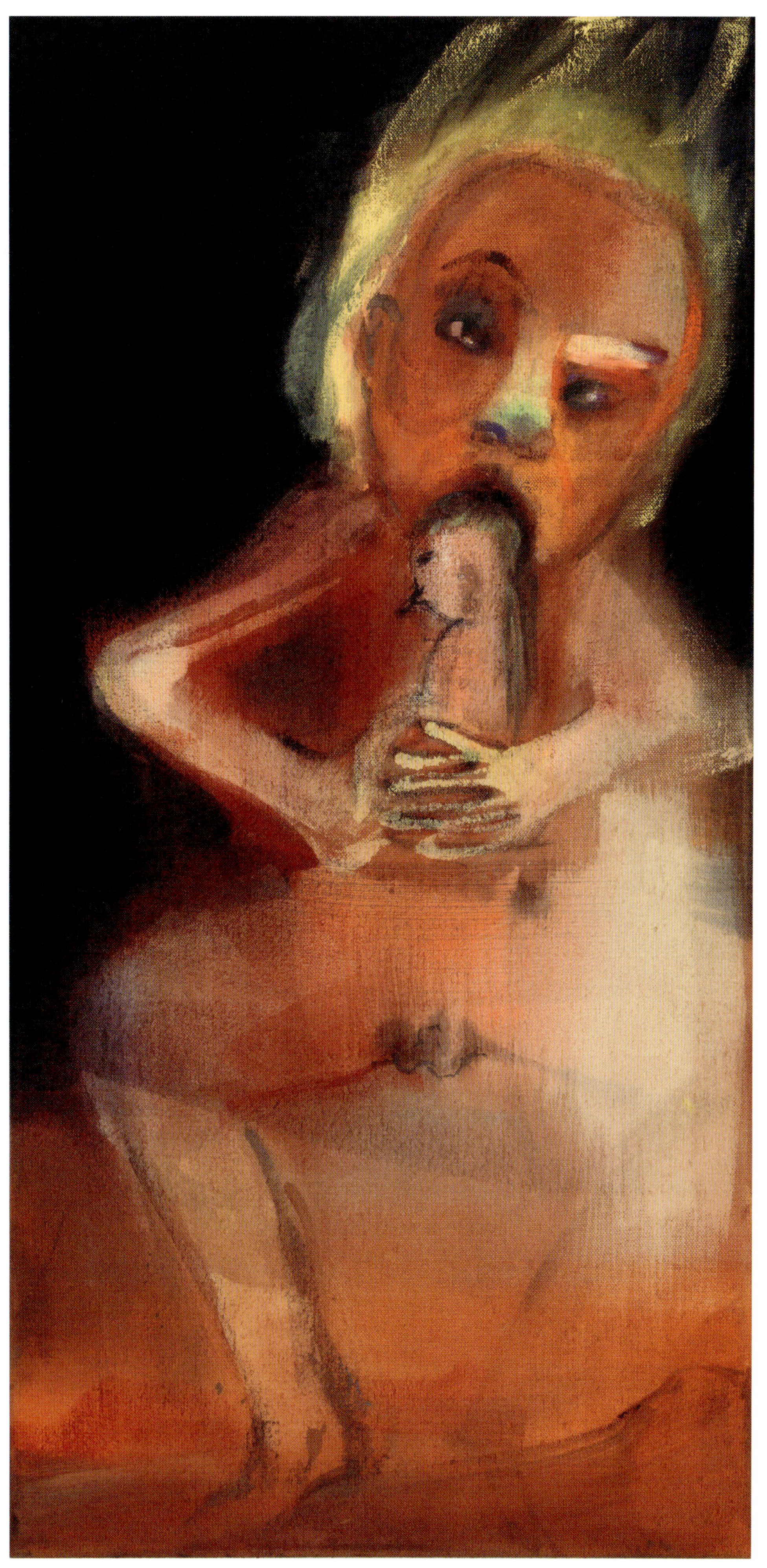

Goyesca, 2015 (21)

ŒUVRES / WERKE / WORKS

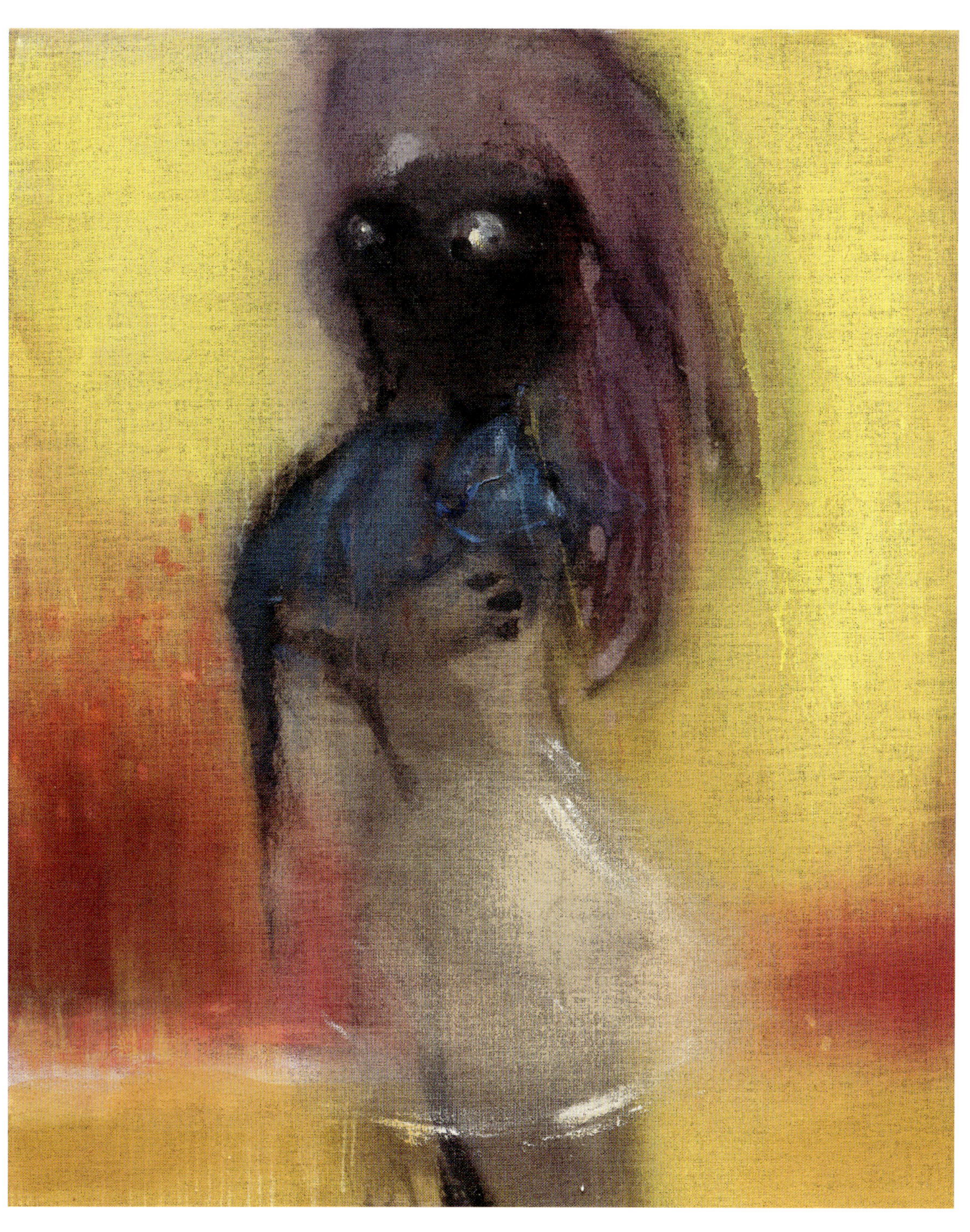

Blue Mom, 2023

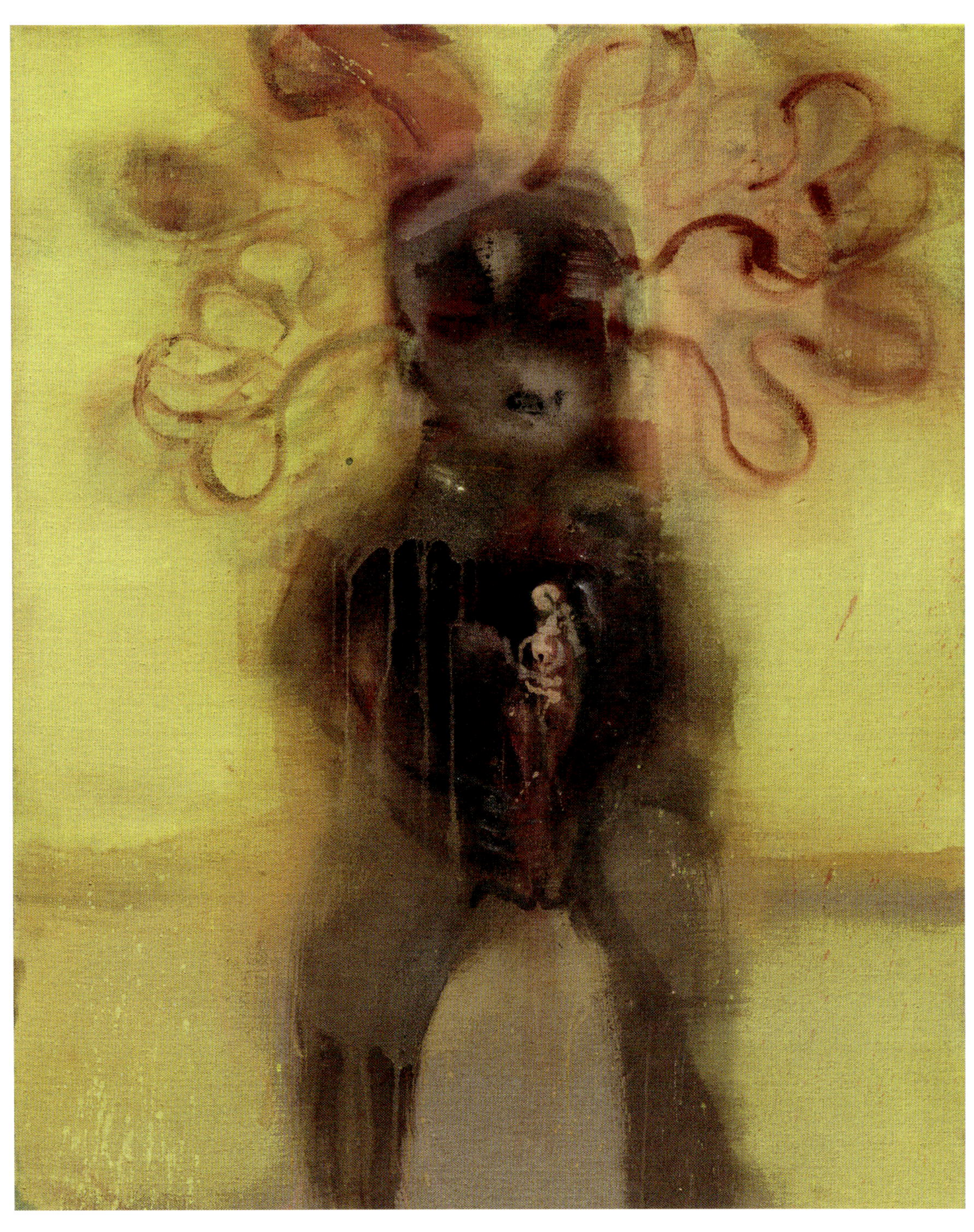

thoughtful, 2023

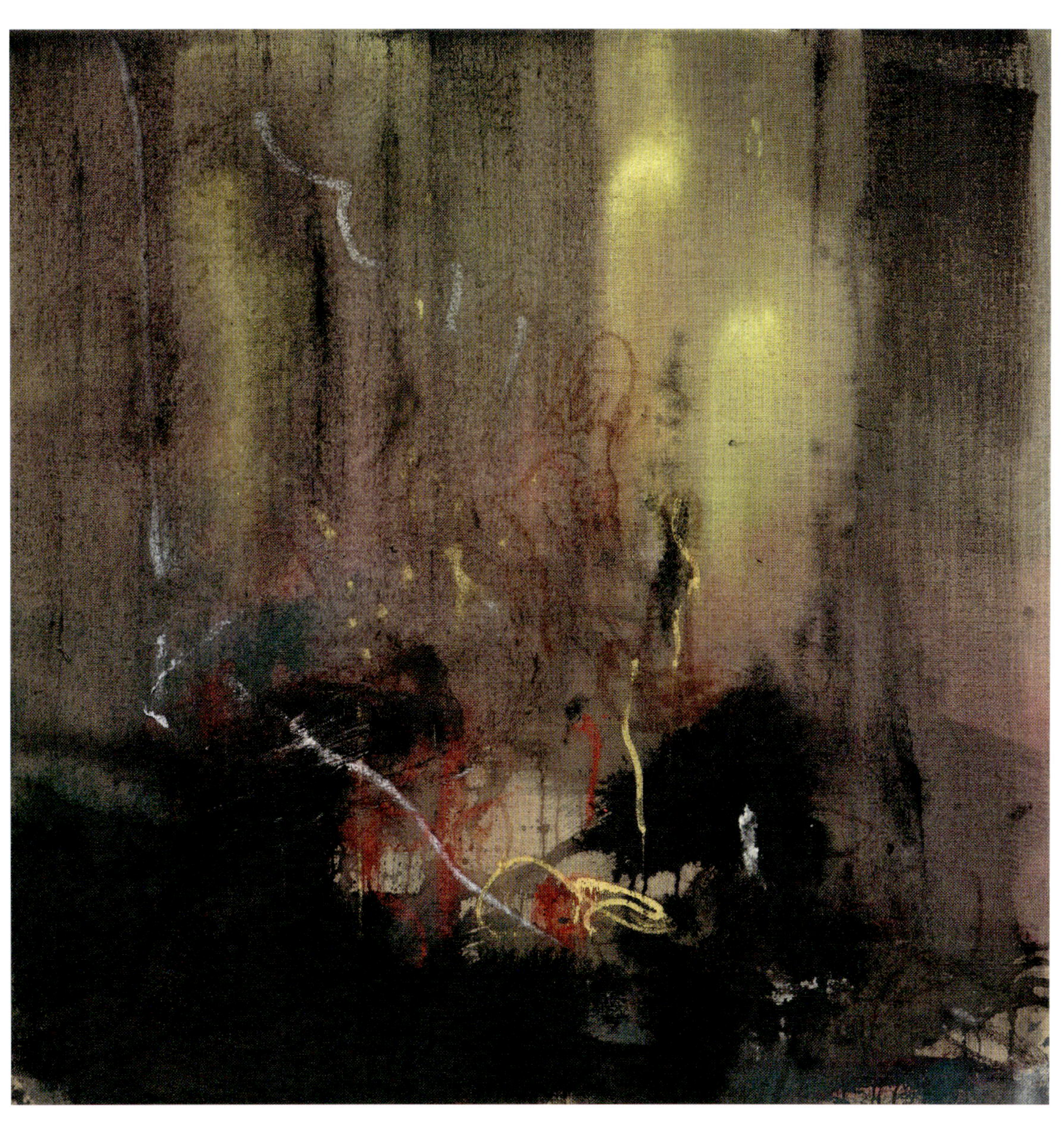

insomnia, 2022

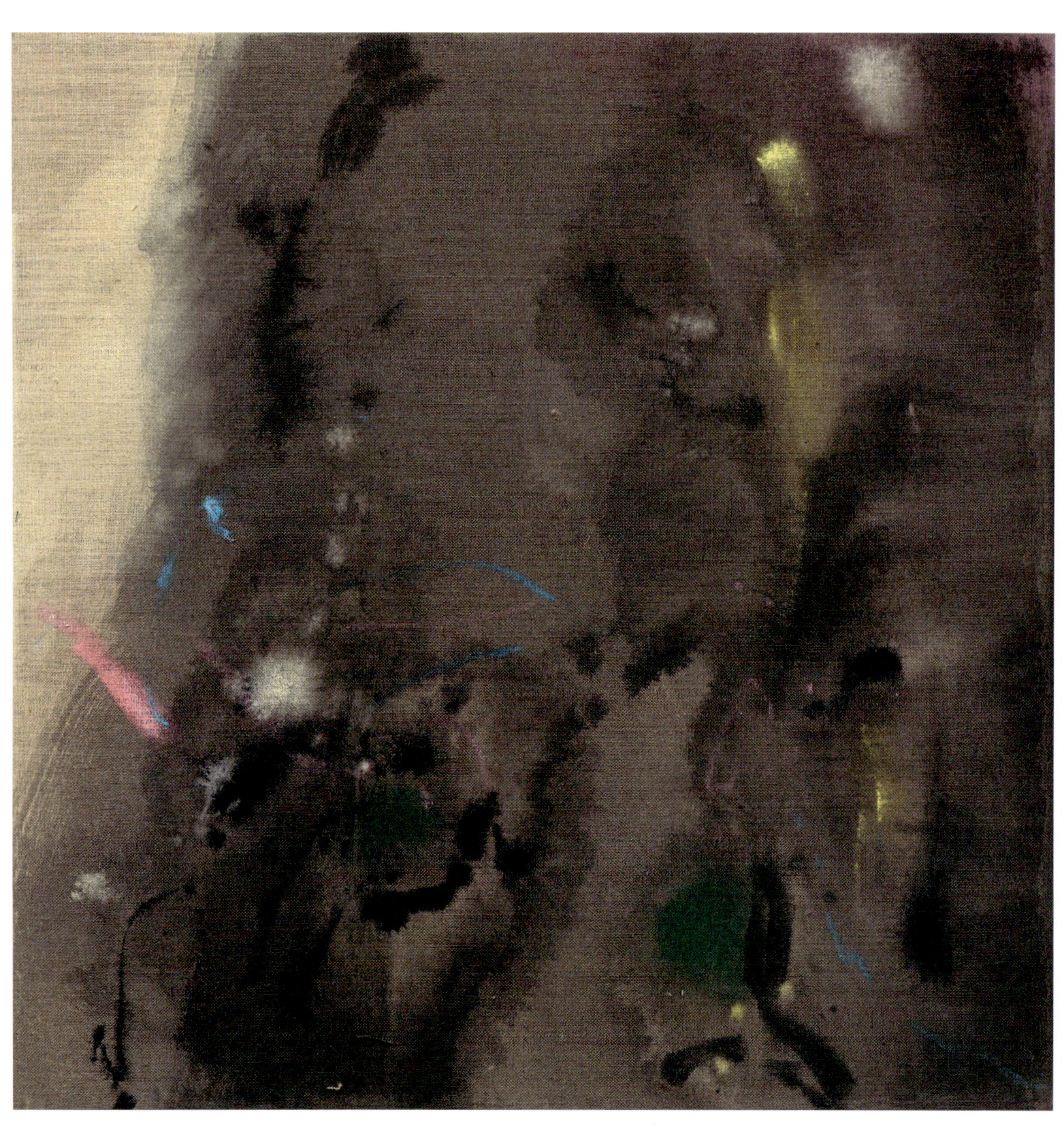

insomnia, 2022

insomnia, 2022
Guernica of our time, 2023 (30–31)

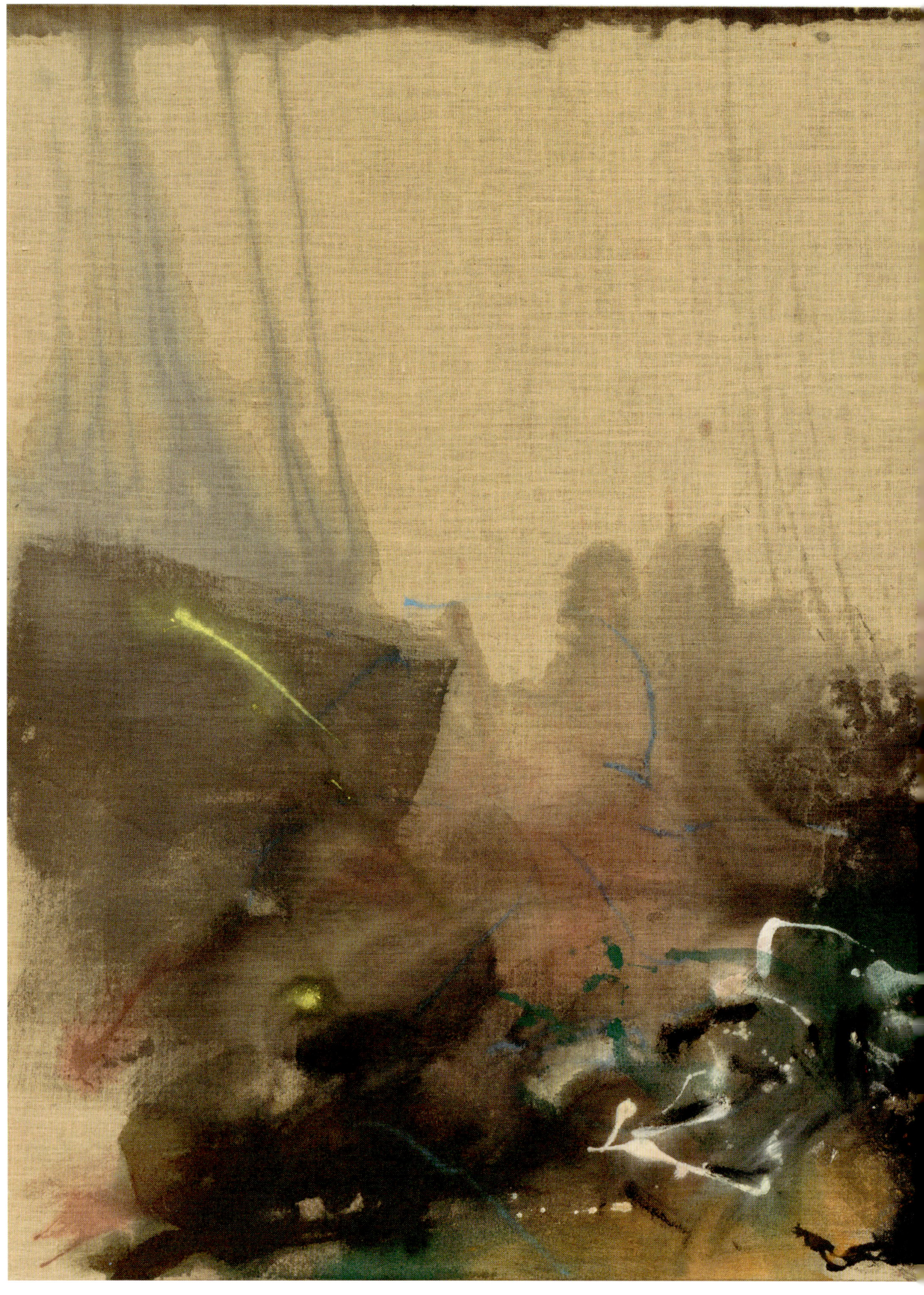

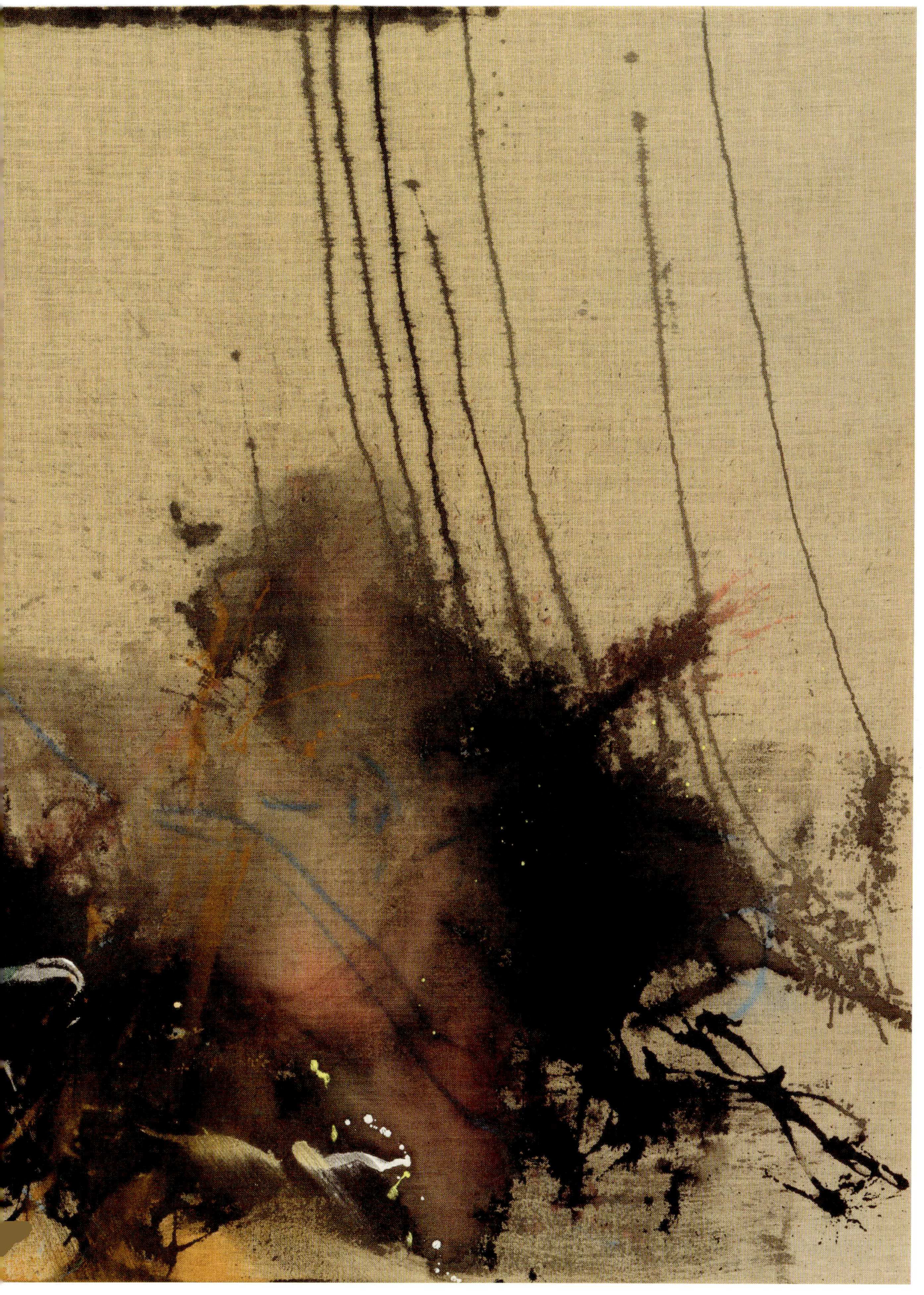

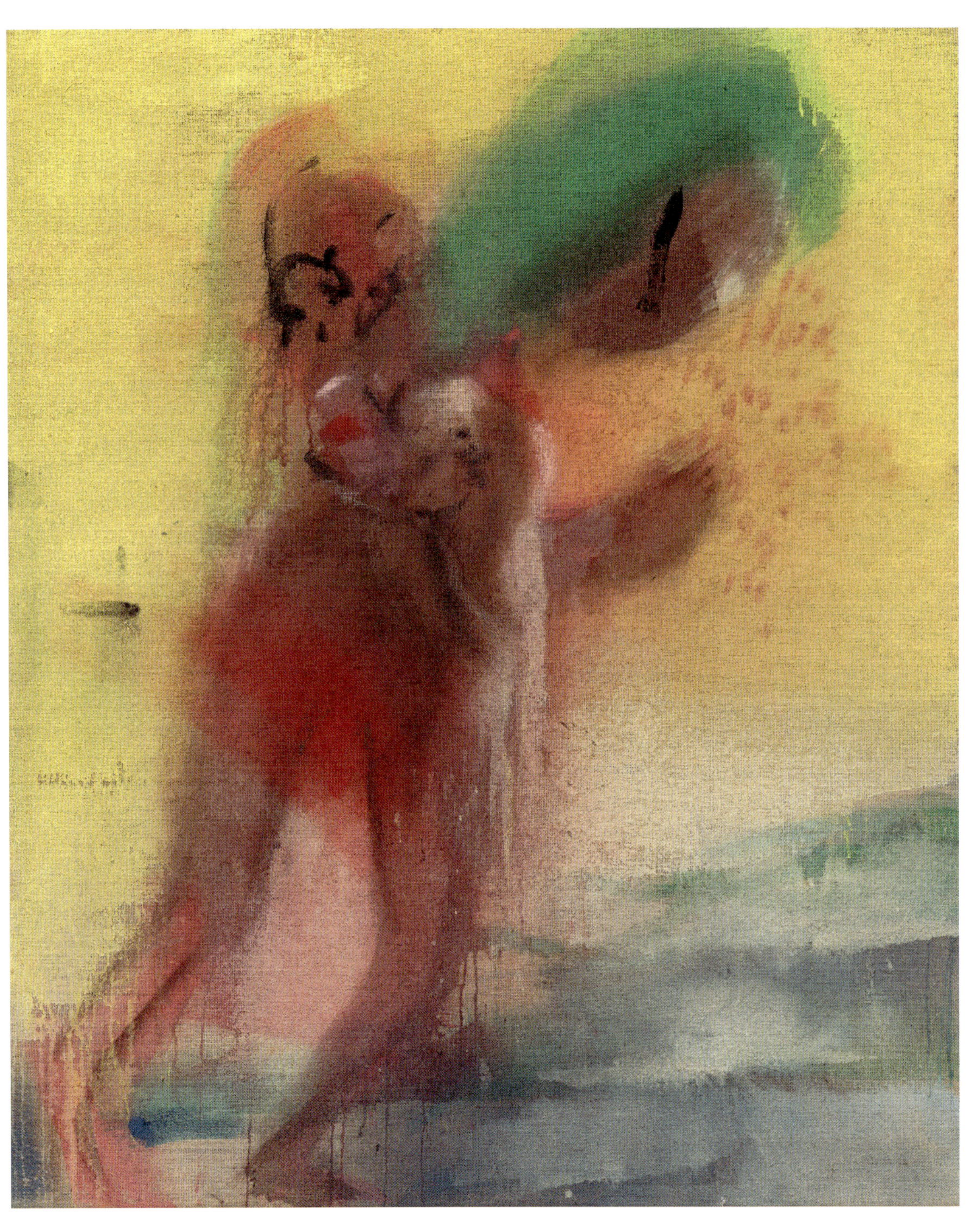

Baby carrying, 2023

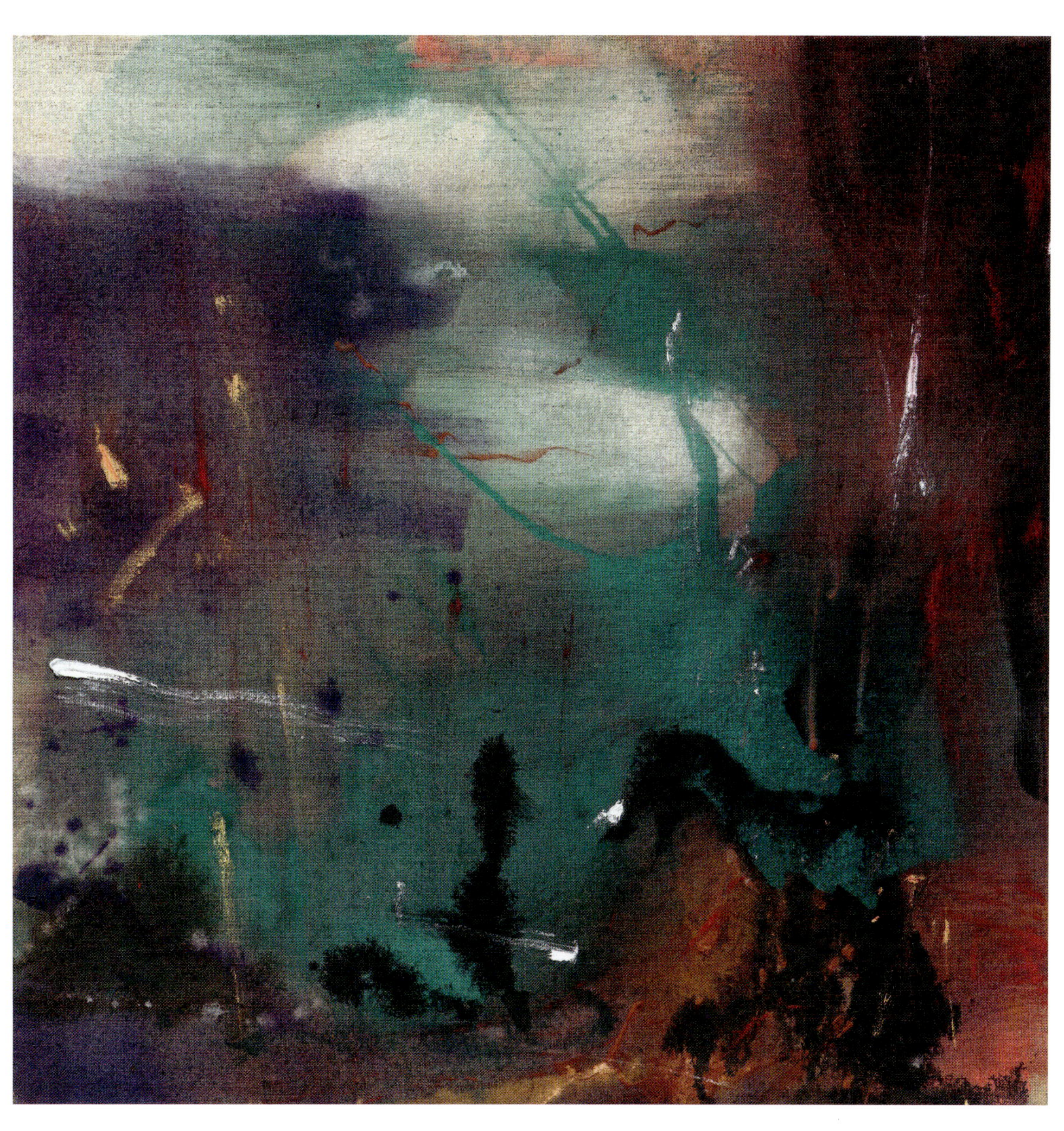

insomnia, 2022

big mom, 2023

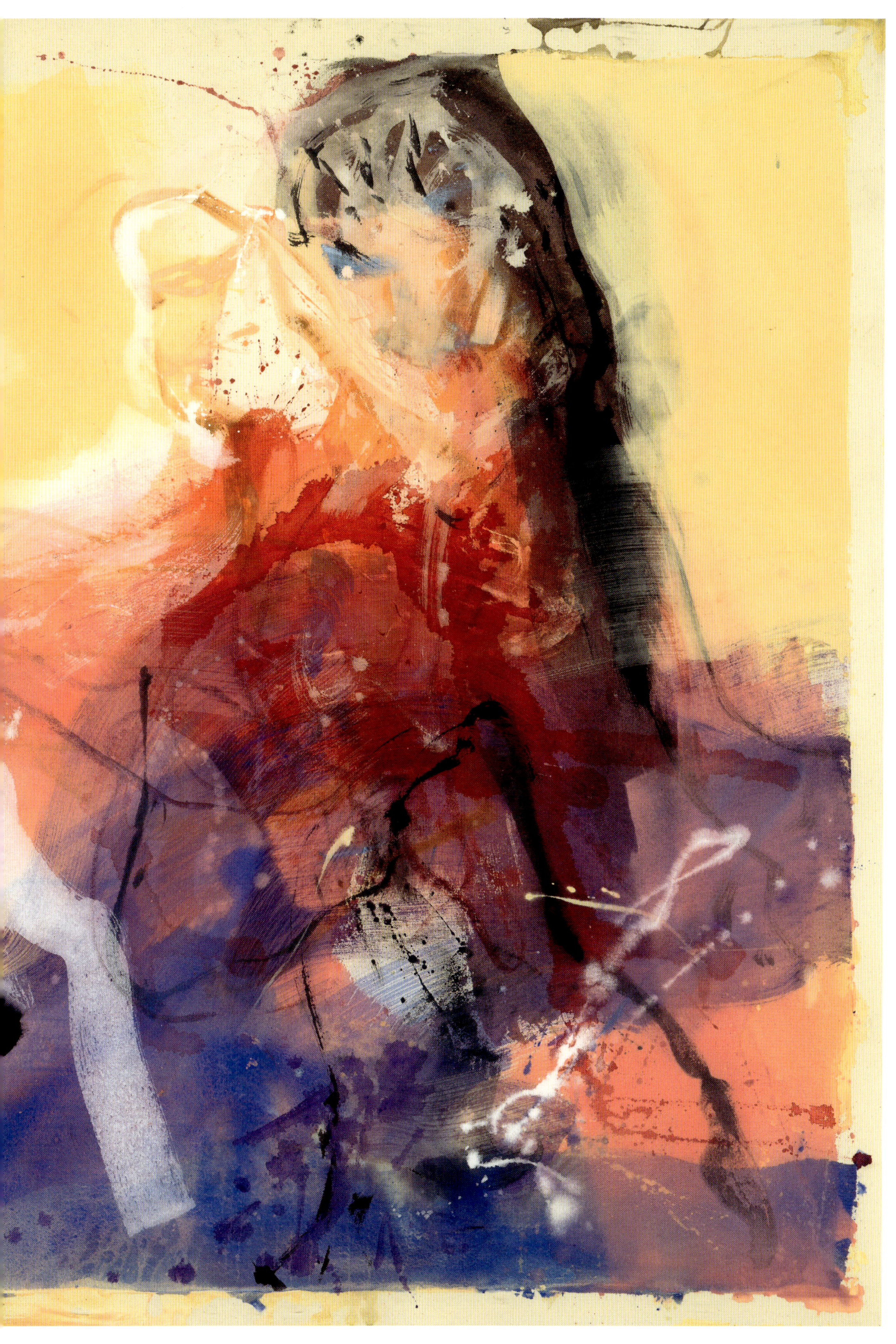

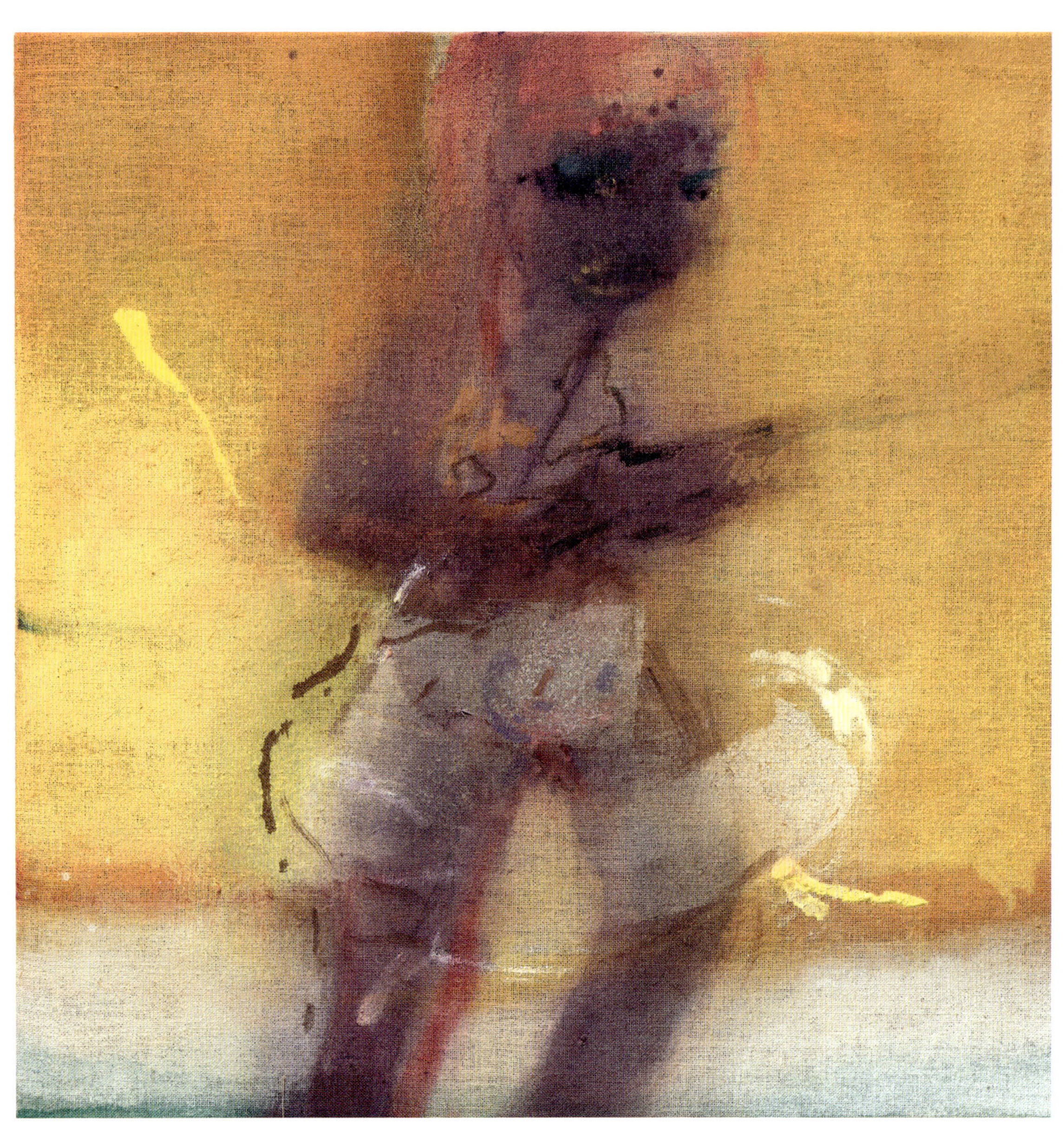

Amazona, 2022

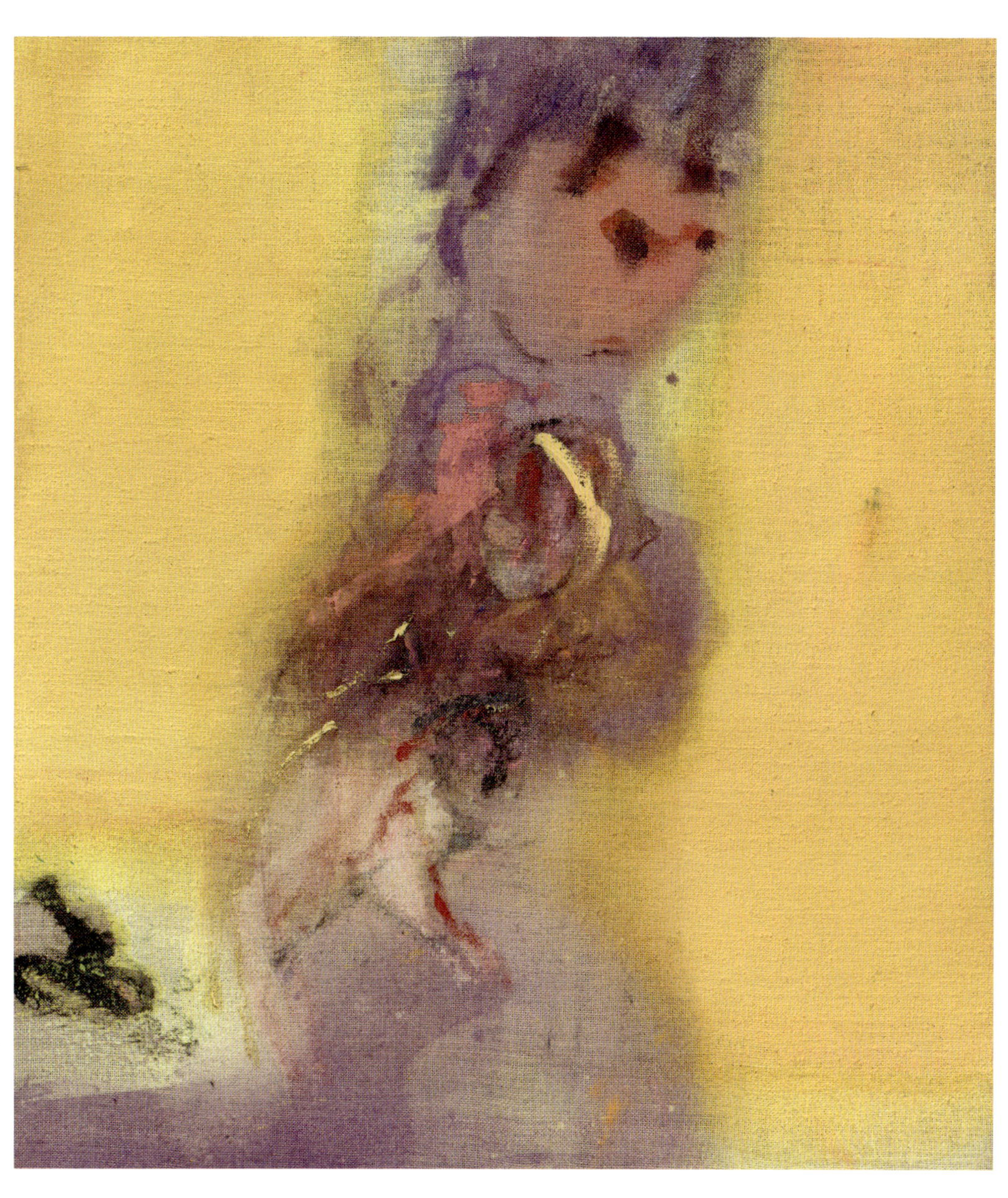

flee free, 2022

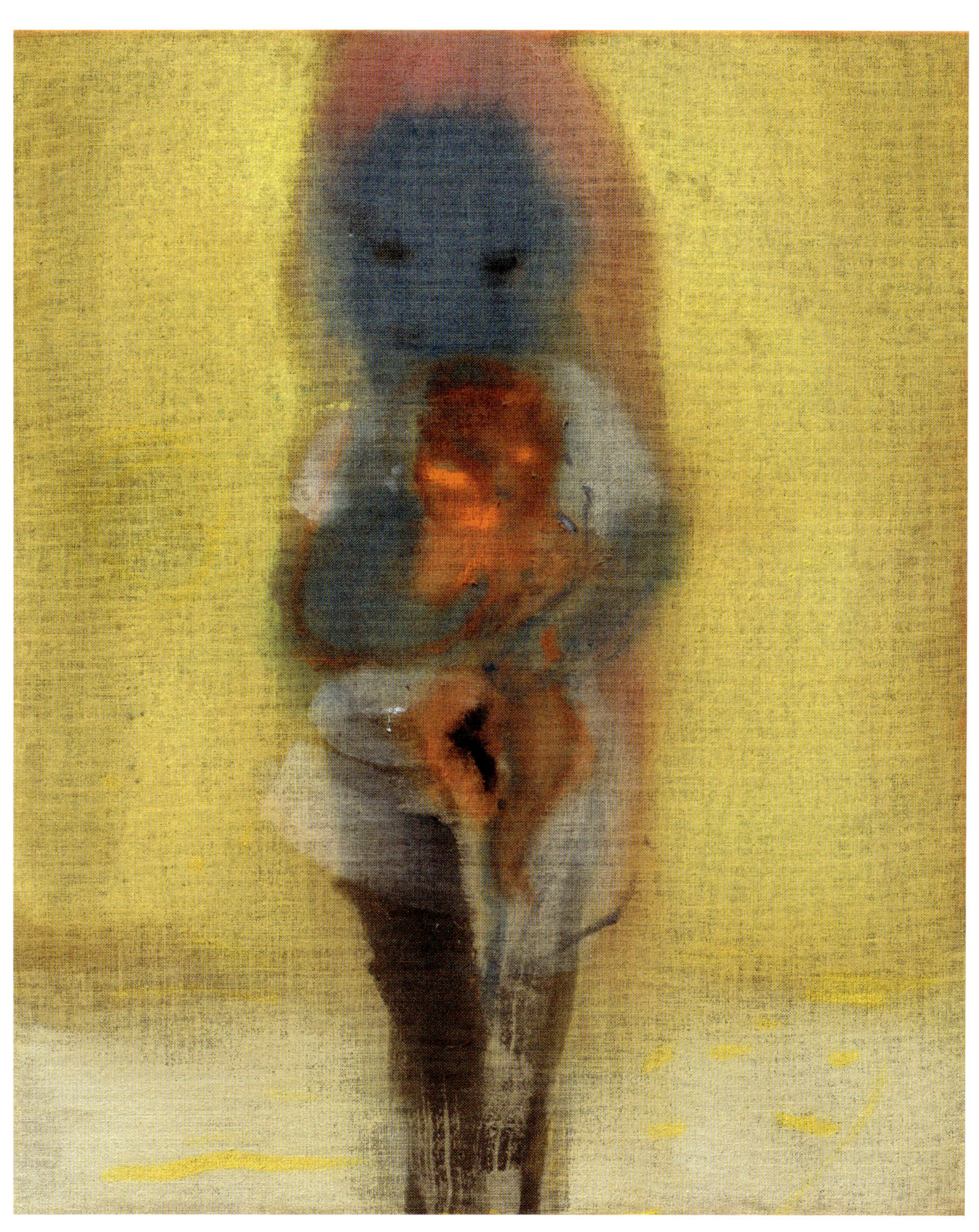

Wedding Girl, 2021

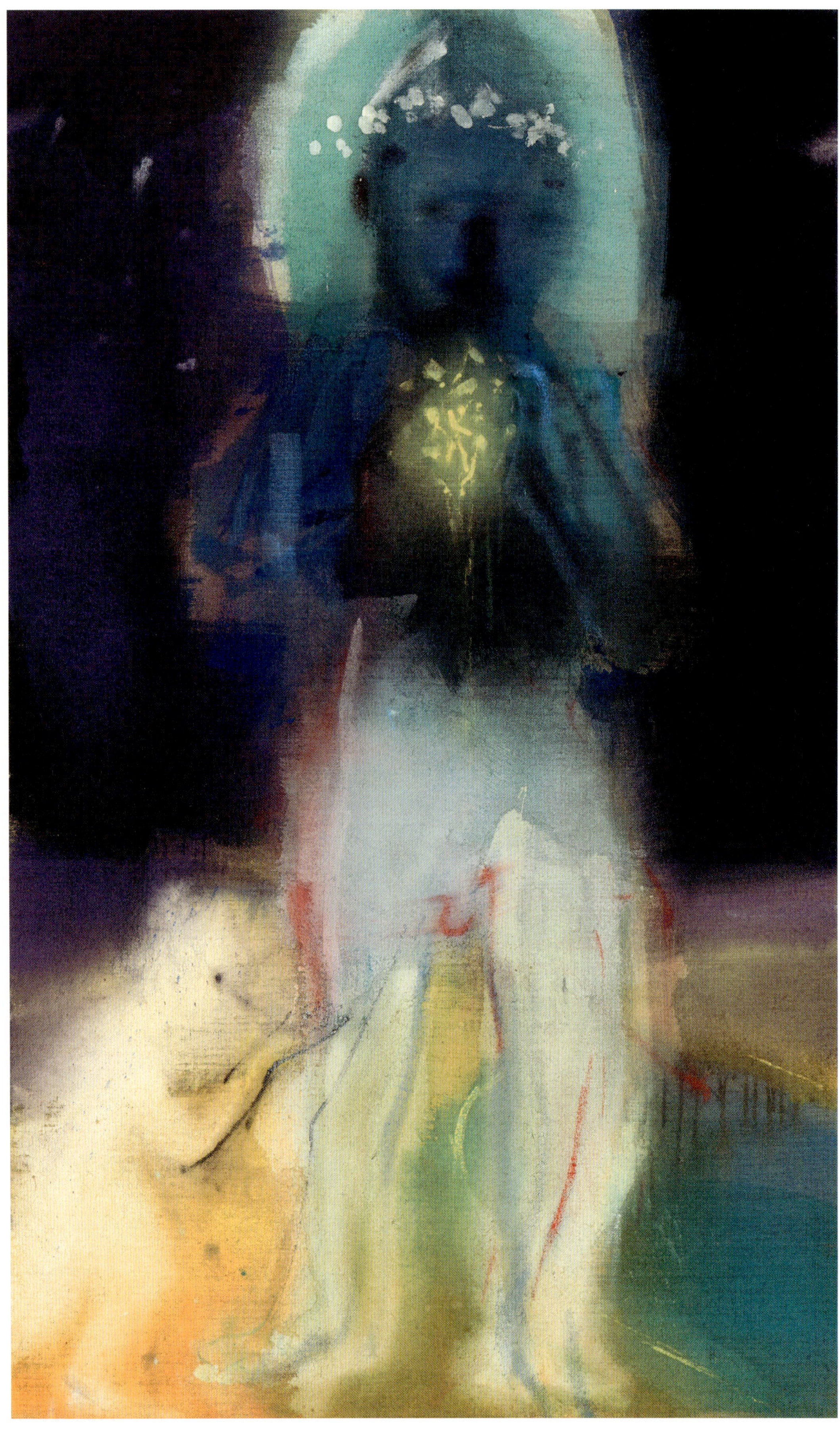

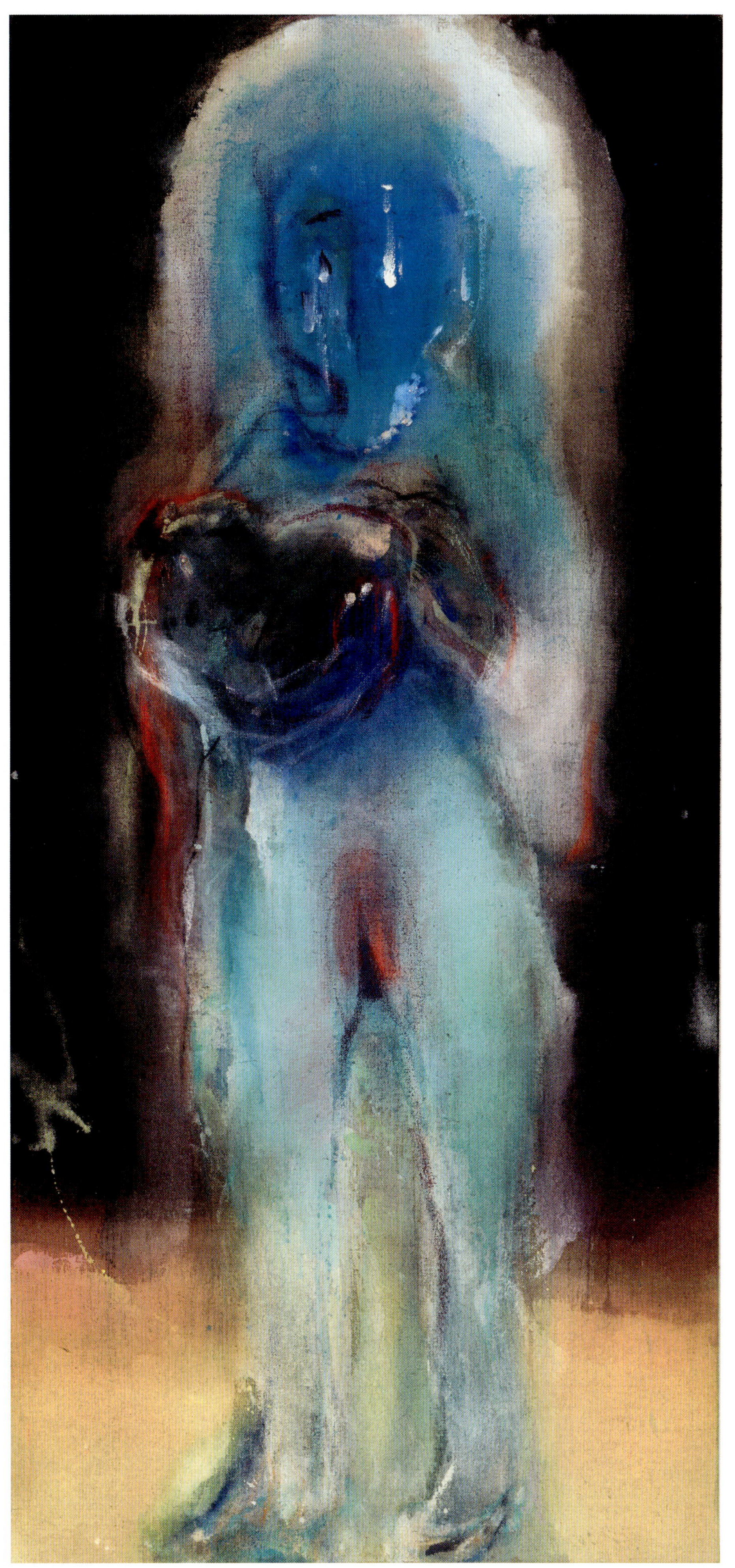

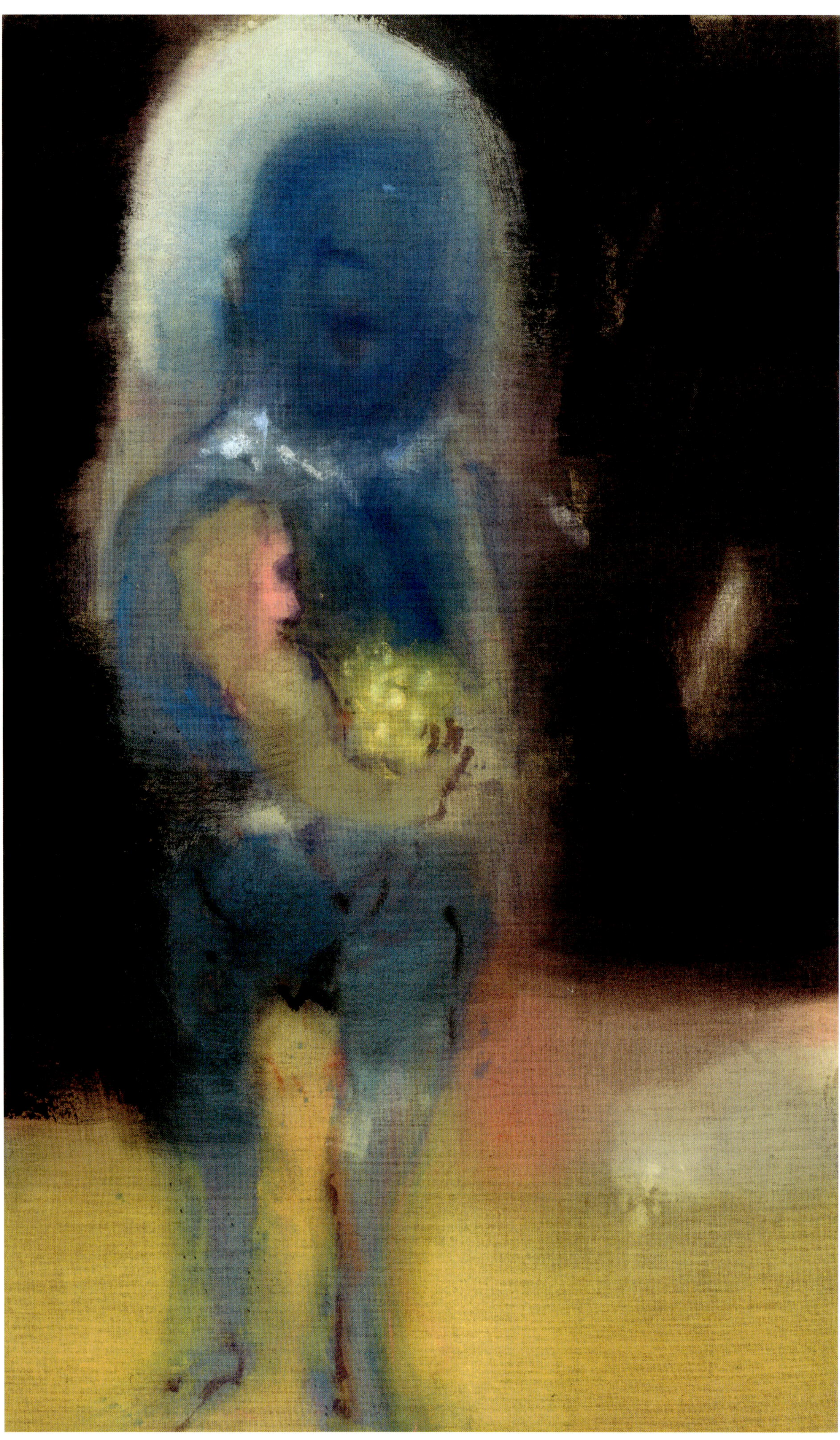

Blue Bride, 2022–23 (40)
Blue Magic, 2022 (41)
Blue Mom, 2023

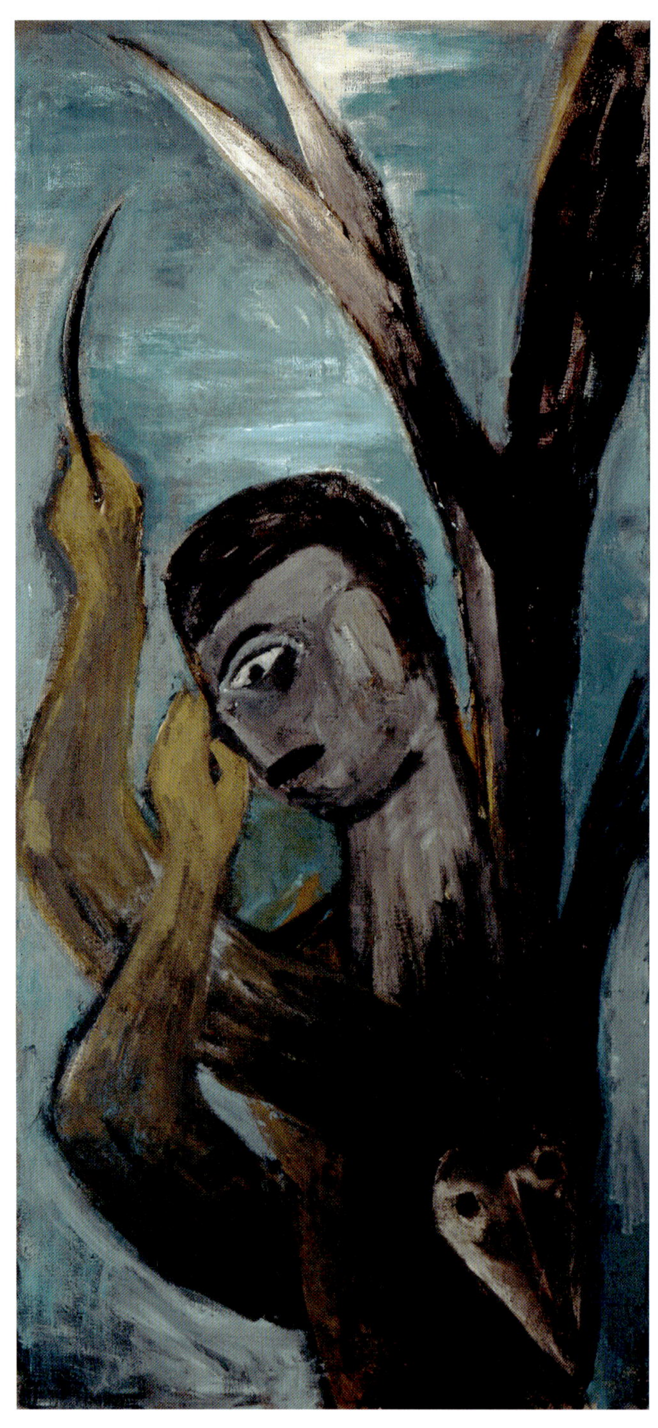

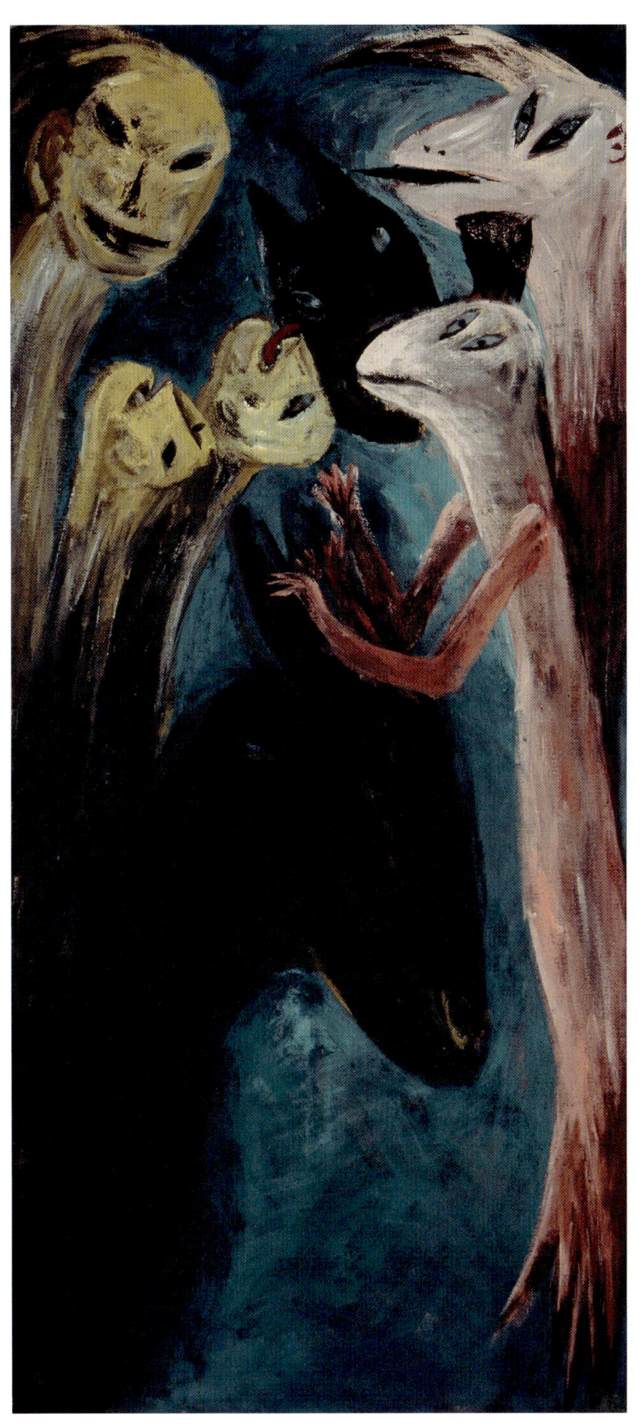
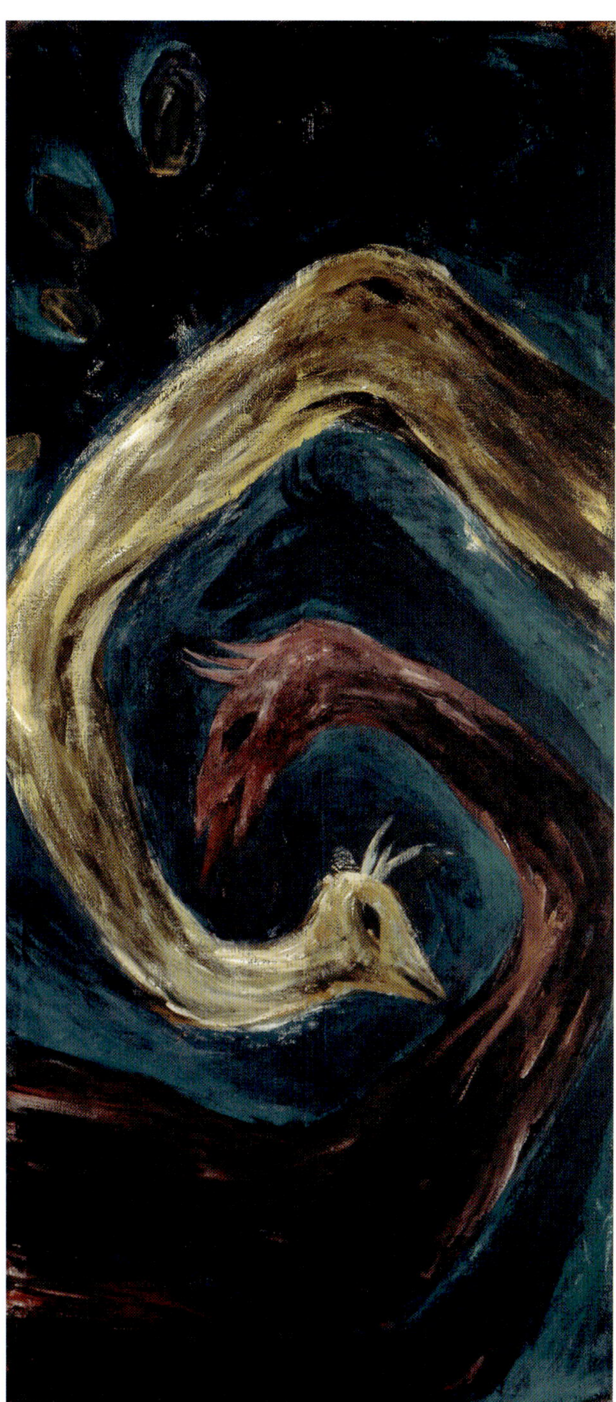

Yokai night, 1985

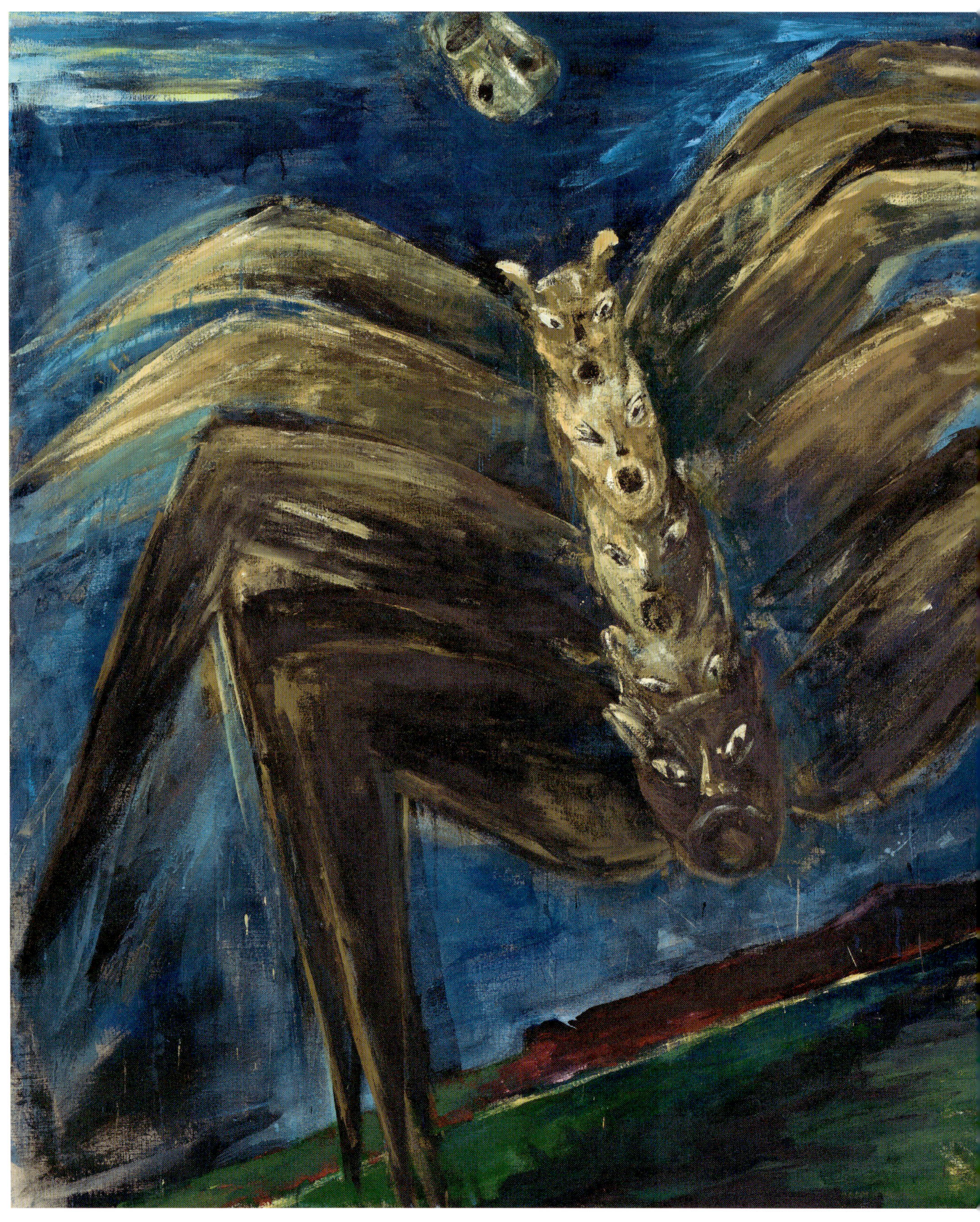

Untitled (Spider), 1980s

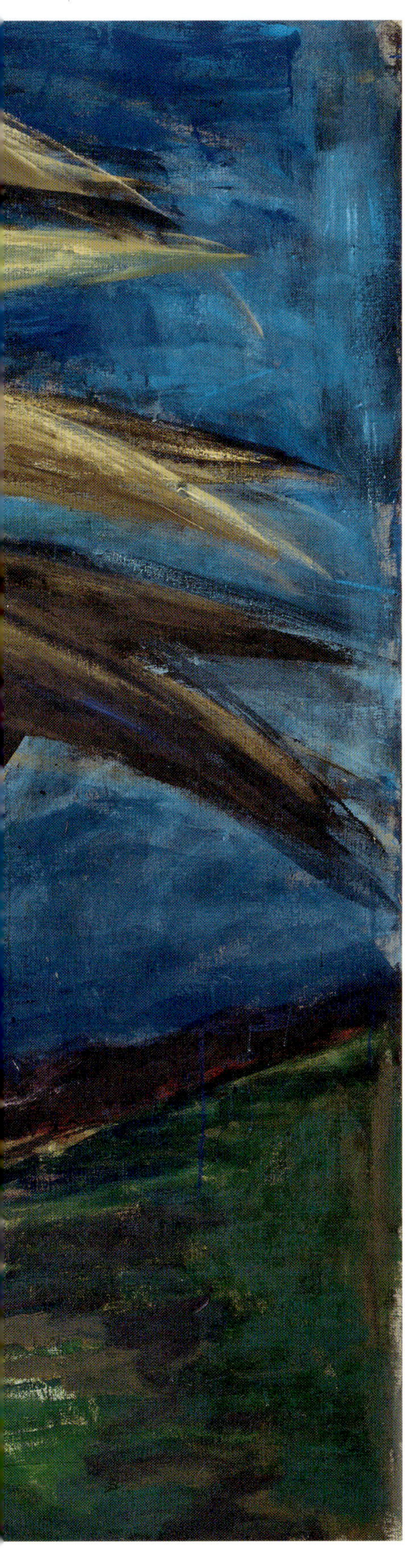

Catgirl with Usagi, 2022 (50–51)

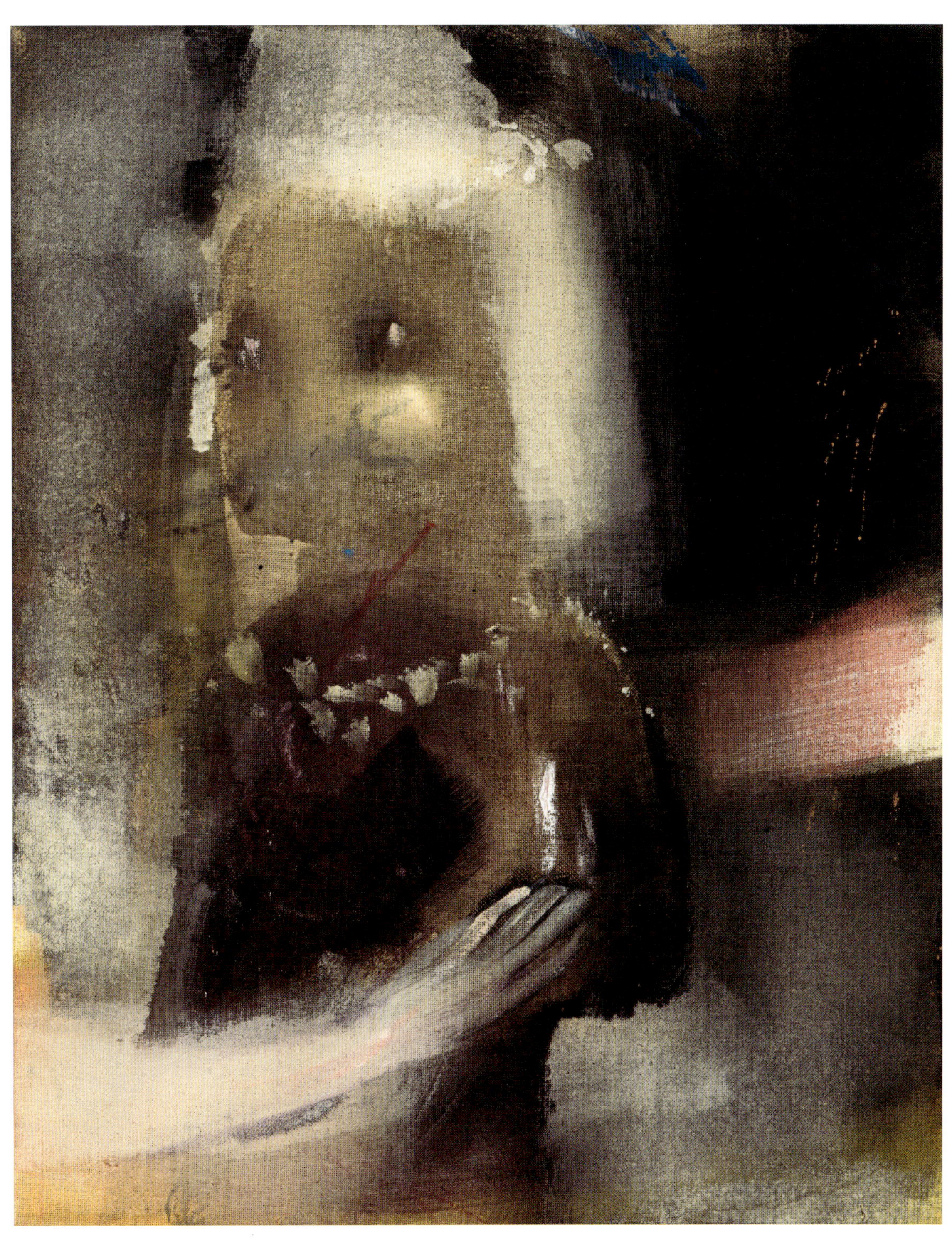

Witch, 2023

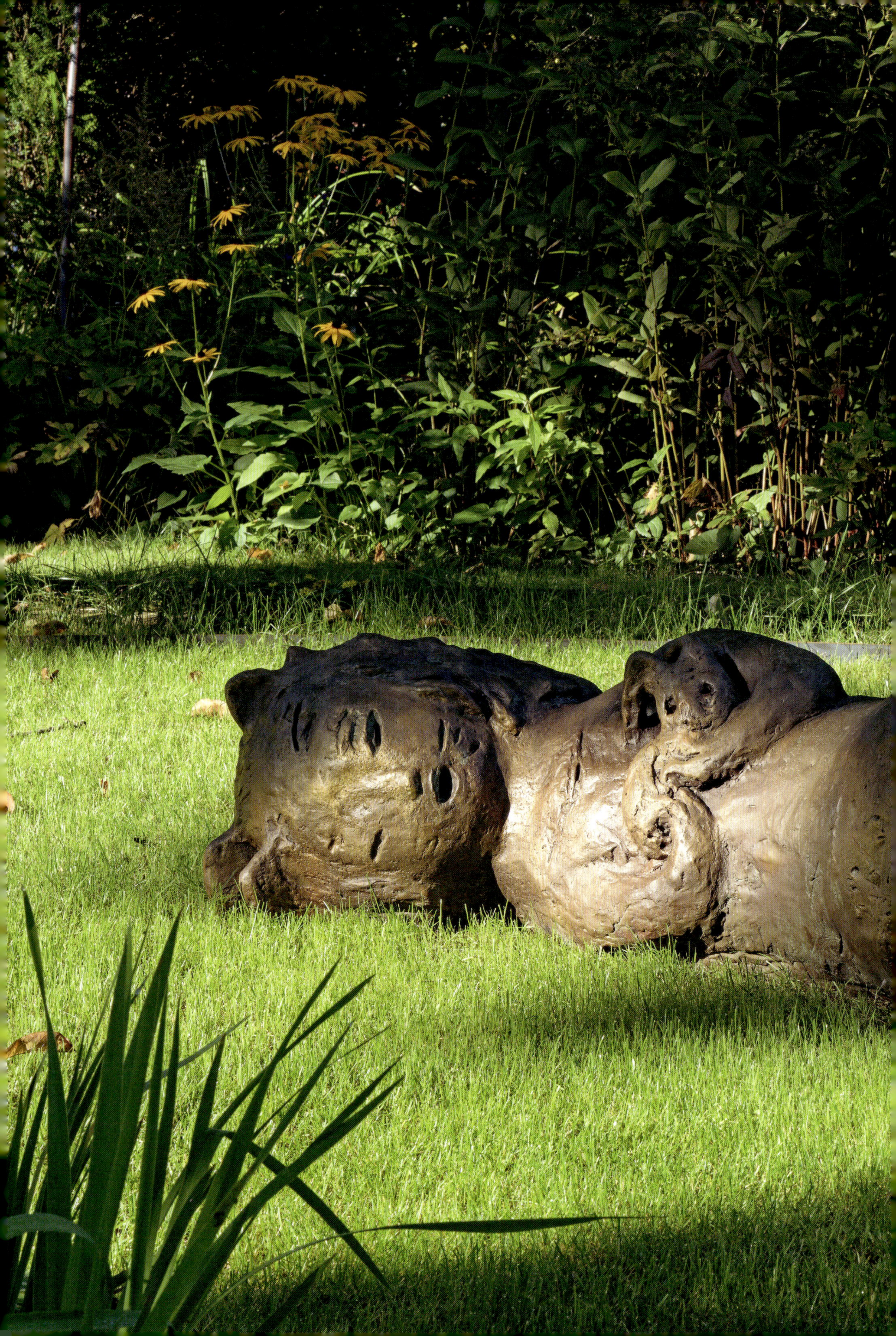

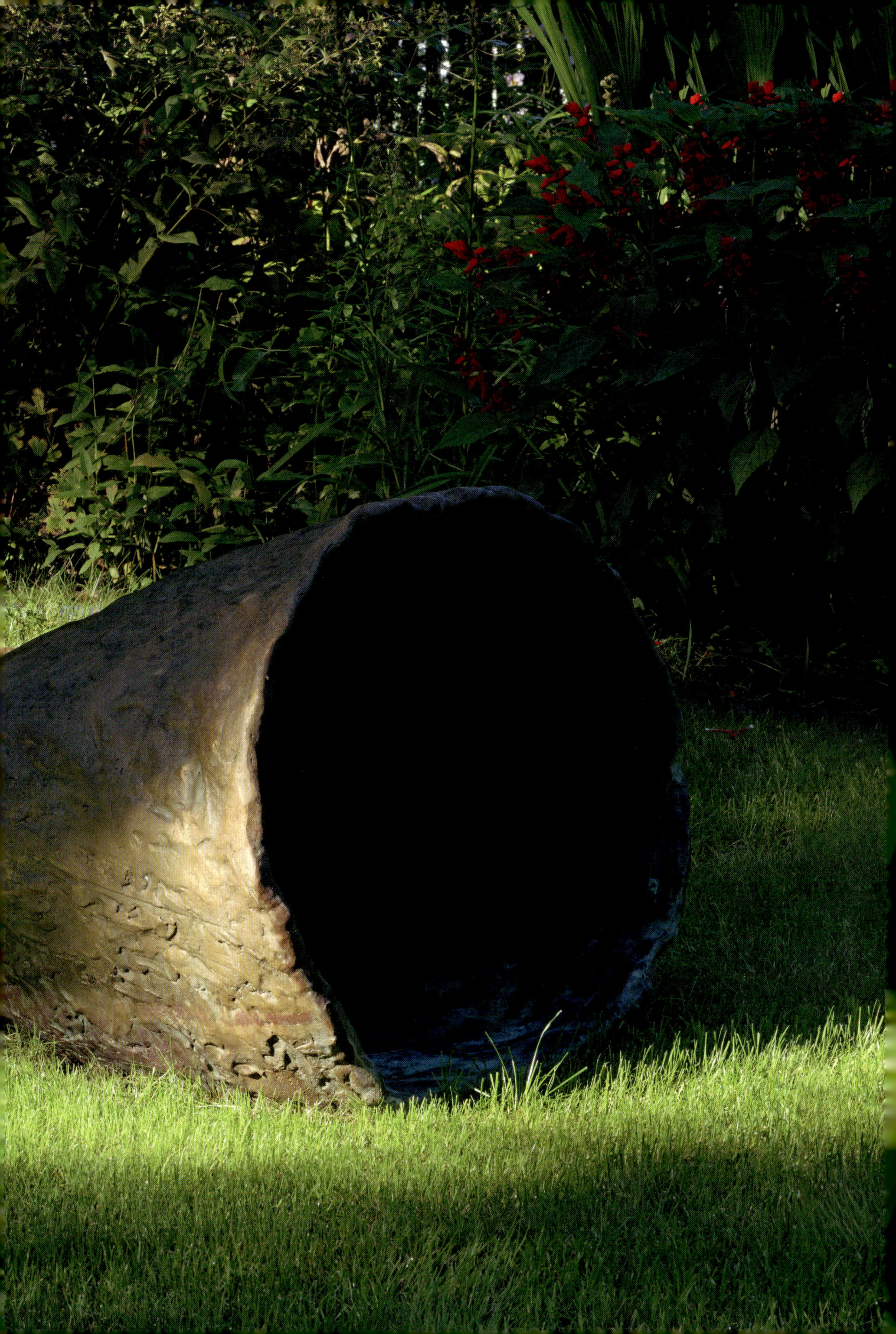

LISTE DES ŒUVRES
WERKVERZEICHNIS
LIST OF WORKS

1 Birds People, 2018/21
Terracotta, glazed
50 × 19 × 17.5 cm
LI/S 9

4–5 Landing, 1981
Charcoal on paper
149.5 × 223 cm
LI/Z 6

10–11 Yokais, 1983
Charcoal on paper
210 × 480 cm
LI/Z 7

14 Rocket Girl I, 2023
Wax form
90 × 52 × 43 cm
LI/S 10

17 Rocket Girl II, 2023
Wax form
103 × 45 × 64 cm
LI/S 11

21 Goyesca, 2015
Tempera on canvas
100 × 50 cm
LI/M 23

25 Blue Mom, 2023
Tempera and oil on jute
120 × 100 cm
LI/M 42

26 thoughtful, 2023
Tempera and oil on canvas
120 × 100 cm
LI/M 44

27 insomnia, 2022
Tempera and oil on nettle
100 × 100 cm
LI/M 37

28 insomnia, 2022
Tempera and oil on nettle
100 × 100 cm
LI/M 40

29 insomnia, 2022
Tempera and oil on nettle
90 × 90 cm
LI/M 38

30–31 Guernica of our time, 2023
Tempera and oil on nettle
190 × 290 cm
LI/M 24

32 Baby carrying, 2023
Tempera and oil on canvas
120 × 100 cm
LI/M 43

33 insomnia, 2022
Tempera and oil on nettle
100 × 100 cm
LI/M 39

34–35 big mom, 2023
Tempera and oil on nettle
150 × 150 cm
LI/M 41

36 Amazona, 2022
Tempera and oil on nettle
90 × 90 cm
LI/M 28

37 flee free, 2022
Tempera and oil on nettle
90 × 80 cm
LI/M 29

39 Wedding Girl, 2021
Tempera and oil on jute
120 × 100 cm
LI/M 35

40 Blue Bride, 2022–23
Tempera and oil on nettle
180 × 110 cm
LI/M 32

41 Blue Magic, 2022
Tempera and oil on nettle
210 × 100 cm
LI/M 30

42 Blue Mom, 2023
Tempera and oil on nettle
180 × 110 cm
LI/M 31

44–45 Yokai night, 1985
Acrylics on canvas
247 x 350 cm each
LI/M 22

46–47 Untitled (Spider), 1980s
Acrylics on canvas
210 × 240 cm
LI/M 21

49 Witch, 2023
Tempera and oil on canvas
100 × 80 cm
LI/M 34

50–51 Catgirl with Usagi, 2022
Bronze patinated
68 × 74 × 160 cm
LI/S 6

This catalogue is published as part of the exhibition

LEIKO IKEMURA
MOMSTARS
16 March – 20 April 2024

Contemporary Fine Arts, Berlin
Bruno Brunnet & Nicole Hackert
Grolmanstraße 32/33
10623 Berlin, Germany
Tel. +49 (0) 30-88 77 71 67
www.cfa-gallery.com
gallery@cfa-berlin.de

Text
Anaël Pigeat

Translation
Stefan Barmann (F/G)
Charles Penwarden (F/E)

Design
Leiko Ikemura
Contemporary Fine Arts, Berlin
Studio Claus Due

Photography
Nick Ash
Jörg von Bruchhausen
Lea Gryze
Leiko Ikemura
Roman März
Lothar Schnepf

Published and produced by
Snoeck Verlagsgesellschaft mbH
Postfach 130217
50496 Köln
www.snoeck.de

ISBN
978-3-86442-435-9

Printed in Germany